Cars of the
Sensational '60s

©2006 Dan Lyons
Published by

krause publications
An Imprint of F+W Publications

700 East State Street • Iola, WI 54990-0001
715-445-2214 • 888-457-2873

Our toll-free number to place an order or obtain
a free catalog is (800) 258-0929.

Library of Congress Catalog Number: 2006905830

ISBN 13-digit: 978-0-89689-388-7
ISBN 10-digit: 0-89689-388-X

Designed by Paul Birling
Edited by Brian Earnest

Printed in China

Dedication

For the amazing Miss Rebecca, whose potential is as high as a cloudless sky.

Acknowledgments

I'm grateful to all of the owners who allowed me to photograph the beautiful cars and trucks found in this book:

Jess & Rita Ruffalo, Les Bowen, Dennis & Gale Kelly, Joseph Carey, Paul Youngs, Isabella Montague, Jim Ferron, Michael Mastrangelo, Mark Mastrangelo, R. Joseph Giolito, Tony Esposito, Frank Esposito, James Cantarella, Dominick Tucci, Bert Roy, John J. Lynch, James & Ruth Wilson, Chuck Goode, John Richmond, Dick Sweeny, Frank Casatelli, John Reichard, Jed Binder, Barry Poet, Duane Goodman, Don Goodrich, Ken Anderson, Sam Cannato, John Kepich, Karl Nippert, Larry & Loretta Swedberg, Howard & Kathleen Phelps, Darryl Peck, Joe Carfagna, Edward Keppner, Bud Congrove, Ralph Butler, Wilbur Groesbeck, Ralph Tomlin, Ed Koehler, Adrian Brooks, John Stanley, Mike Moore, Mike Rice, Jim Boniello, Marty Greany, Lindsay Carte, Jarvis Barton, Fred Scheer, Dave & Cindy Keetch, Tom Manganello, Dave Goodwin, Ray Elias, Don McLennan, Edith & Parker Wickham, James O'Bryan, Jim Jackson, Glenn & Sandy Hutchinson, Joe Verrillo, Joe James, Dean Kelley, Ron Perry, Les Bent, Kevin Kolvenbach, Ron Pearson, Gary Sommers, Jack Sager and Rich Rosetti.

Cars of the Sensational '60s / Contents

1960-69 Chevy Corvette

F ew cars went through more changes than Corvette in the 1960s. It entered the decade running out the string on the classic, first-generation cars that stretched from 1953-1962. From 1960-64, these small-block, solid-axle 'Vettes were stars of the small screen. The Route 66 television show featured Martin Milner and George Maharis as two young guys cruising the country in search of ratings in a brand new Corvette.

The years from 1963-67 brought wholesale changes. These "C-2" cars were destined to become Corvette's most popular era, and the most collectible. The product of stylist Bill Mitchell, the '63-'67 Corvette Sting Rays were shorter, lower and more sleek than past Corvettes. A sharply creased beltline defined the lines of the car, neatly wrapping around its entirety. The knife-edge front

▲ *1961 was the last year of availability for a contrasting cove color on the Corvette, though the buyer of this Roman Red roadster resisted the urge.*

◄ *The revamped tail end on the '61 Corvette was a rear view preview of the upcoming second-generation cars.*

Striking, split window coupes ▲ *were a one-year wonder, replaced by a one-piece backlight the following year.*

A fuel-injected, 360-hp/327-cid was ▶ *the rarest and most powerful motor in the '63 Corvette lineup. Twelve percent of Corvette buyers ponied up the extra $430.40 for a "fuelie."*

A Beige interior was a ▶ *perfect complement to Saddle Tan exterior.*

introduced hideaway headlights — a signature styling theme in Corvettes for 40 years hence. The back end kept the dual light, ducktail look previewed in 1961. The rear view got especially interesting in a new body style. A hardtop coupe took its place alongside the traditional roadster in the Corvette lineup. Mitchell's design called for the two rear windows to be divided by a center strip. An uninterrupted line would then follow the flow of the stylistic spine, running north to south. The result was the collector cherished "split window coupe." all the more desirable because it lasted for just one year. Grumblings over reduced rear visibility eventually convinced Chevy to replace the rear view with a one-piece backlight, and so it stayed for the remainder of the second generation.

INSTANT CELEBRITY

The car you drive reflects who you are to the world. Aside from its dramatic looks and vivid performance, the new Corvette Sting Ray imparts an aura of individuality to its owner. Why? Because the Corvette Sting Ray has its own vibrant personality—but more important, because it's a uniquely different kind of car, as personal as your monogram. Tailored to the true privacy of two-passenger travel. No committees.

And you can equip your Sting Ray to suit your own driving habits. A complete list of extra-cost options includes power steering, power brakes, power windows, radio, and automatic transmission. Plus engine choices up to 360 hp. You can expect a subtle extra measure of attention and respect when you drive a Corvette Sting Ray.... Chevrolet Division of General Motors, Detroit 2, Michigan.

NEW CORVETTE STING RAY BY CHEVROLET

With the updated looks came upgraded mechanics. Most notably new was independent rear suspension. This bit of chassis sophistication was unique for the day, and consistent with the race-oriented philosophy of Corvette Chief Engineer Zora Arkus-Duntov. A parade of performance motors passed under the bonnets of Corvettes during this era. Everything from fuel-injected small blocks to the first big block motors was wrapped in fiberglass.

Chevy rang out the '60s with a third-generation of Corvette, starting in 1968. The radical design was inspired by the 1965 Mako Shark II concept car. The swoopy, shark-like shape would prove to have unusually long legs, lasting with minor modifications through 1982. Though the styling was new and controversial, beneath the skin, C-3 Corvettes were largely holdovers from the previous generation. Corvettes of this period were witness to everything from the halcyon days of the muscle car era to the dark days of the energy crisis and beyond. As a result, the veteran chassis held a succession of engines during its tenure. Small- and big-block motors in a variety of pavement

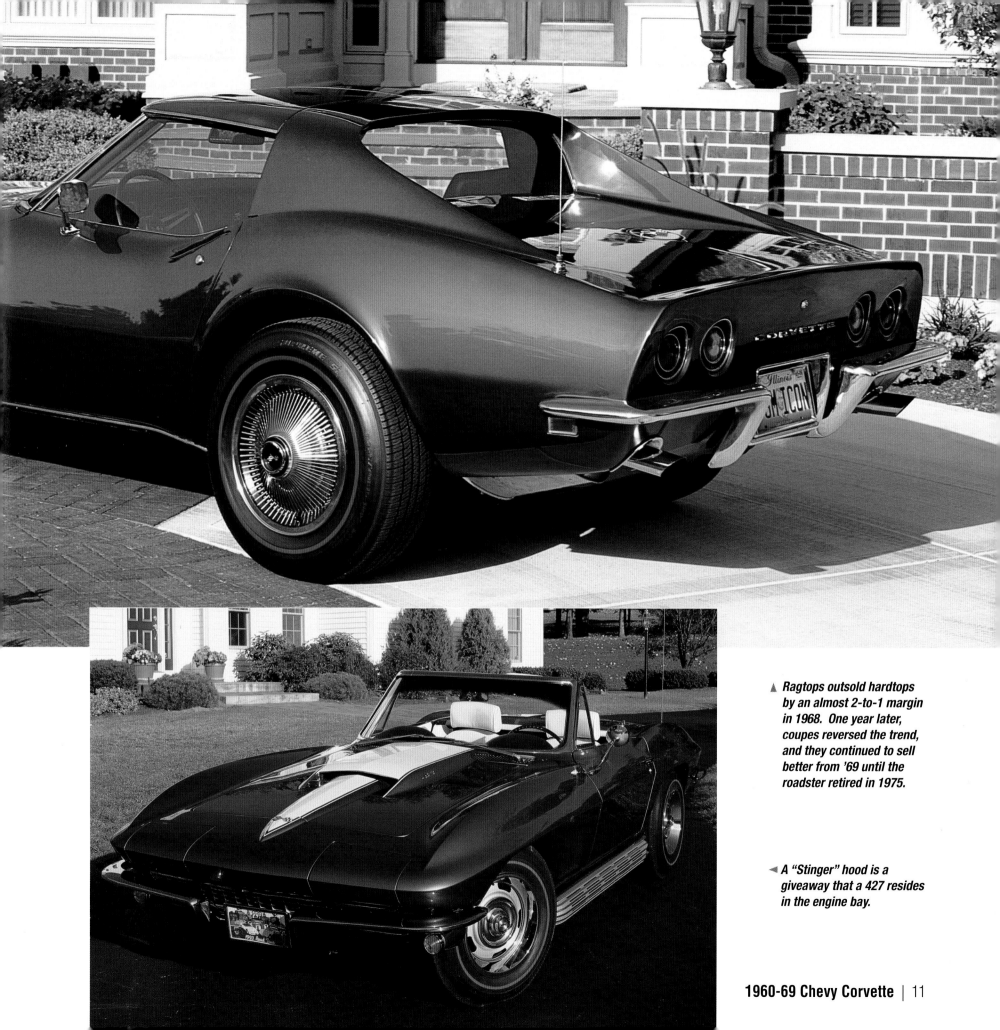

▲ Ragtops outsold hardtops by an almost 2-to-1 margin in 1968. One year later, coupes reversed the trend, and they continued to sell better from '69 until the roadster retired in 1975.

◄ A "Stinger" hood is a giveaway that a 427 resides in the engine bay.

punishing trims were available to all in the late '60s. But as the 1970s dawned, performance regressed, rapidly chased off the option charts by energy and insurance concerns.

Such were the design cycles of Corvette that the 1960s would lay claim to parts of three of the fiberglass flyer's most significant eras. Each was stylistically unique, each had its champions and critics, yet all were part of a common chain that links Corvettes to this day.

Looking back, it's hard to think of any American car that evolved further, faster than Corvette in the 1960s.

▲ The last year of the decade was easily the best year for Corvette sales. Production of 38,762 in '69 compared with 10,261 in 1960.

◄ Only 13 percent of all 1966 Corvette buyers opted for the $101.65 side mount exhaust system.

1960-62 Chrysler 300 Letter Cars

From the mid-1950s to the mid-'60s, Chrysler's hot rod halo cars were the 300 Letter Series: full-size, limited-build land bombs that set the performance tone for the division. The three-year period from 1960-62 was pivotal for the 300 series, as these cars transitioned from finned, '50s fliers to a more contemporary shape. They also reached the highest horsepower and performance levels that the series would ever see. And finally, they paved the way for their ultimate departure. As the 300 series eventually became mainstream, the performance torch was passed on to Plymouth and Dodge.

Each year, the 300s had a different sequential letter in their name, and by 1960, the alphabetic tally was up to "F." These models were a mix of the old and the new. From the outside, Chrysler was still in

▲ *The new, rounded rear profile on '62 Chryslers was handsome and modern looking.*

◄ *Chrysler re-christened the former Windsor line the 300 Sport in 1962, thus marking the first time a non-letter series car would carry the numerical name.*

its late tailfin phase, though some other manufacturers had already moved away from that look. Up front, quad headlights straddled a broad, blacked-out trapezoidal grille. Out back, the trunk lid was "decorated" by spare tire carrier imprint, which many thought had an uncanny resemblance to a toilet seat. Underneath the skin, the 300 rolled on an all-new, unit body chassis. The basic engine in the 300F was a 413-cid wedge, pumping out 375 hp. 1960 saw the first manual transmission applications in the 300 series. A scant seven or so 300Fs were fitted with the optional 400-hp motor and Pont-a-Mousson stick. These cars went down to Daytona Beach for Speed Week and promptly kicked sand in the face of the competition, logging record times for the flying mile ranging from 141.5 to 144.9 mph.

In '61, Chrysler was still clinging to tailfins, but there were other style changes afoot up front and in back. The face view was noticeably different. The quad headlights were now canted at about the same angle as the tailfins, and the grille that they book-ended was

▼ Swoopy, red ram induction tubes and gold-crowned carburetors on the 300F draw crowds at car shows every time the hood is raised.

flipped wide side up. Meanwhile, on the deck lid, designers finally took the hint and flushed the toilet seat in favor of a smooth lid. The four speeds were gone from the option list, but in their place was a Chrysler built three-speed manual. However, the vast majority of 300s still drove the durable TorqueFlite three-speed automatic.

The following year was notable for the 300 for three main reasons. Tailfins, found on every Letter Car since '57 were gone; the wings clipped into a rounded, more modern profile. Mechanically, the 300H offered the maximum thrust ever seen in the series. Standard power was supplied by the 380 horsepower 413, and the step-up option bumped the ante to 405 hp. At the same time, Chrysler decided to take advantage of the Letter Car's cache by creating a second, non-letter 300 series. The former, mid-line Windsor series henceforth became known as the 300s.

By 1966, only the non-letter 300s remained. But by then, arguably, Chrysler had made its point. Dodge and Plymouth took up arms against the young muscle car bucks, and the "Elegant Brutes" retired to a very special place in automotive history.

The infamous "toilet seat" was ▲ bracketed by Chrysler's still tall tailfins in 1960.

1960-61 Plymouth Fury

P ity the poor stylist. Designing years in advance of production, they fly blind, trying to predict what will be hot and what will not. Sometimes they get it right. Sometimes they swing and miss.

The 1960 Plymouth was largely designed in 1957, at the height of tailfin popularity. By 1960, fins were losing fans, but the die had already been cast (literally). The new Plymouths emerged, fully finned, to sagging sales. '61 models looked much

different, but ironically, they sold much worse. Total 1960 production of 447,724 units was followed by 349,835 in '61. Fins had been flattened, and to each side of the razed rear deck was affixed a bullet-shaped taillight. The front end proved more controversial. A pair of knitted, chrome brows arched over the headlamps, framing a pinched grille. Overall, it was a mixed result from an aesthetic standpoint; the look compared famously by stylist Virgil Exner to "a plucked chicken." It was different, but buyers were indifferent, registering

▲ *The Fury's rear end was radically reshaped in '61. Tall tailfins were planed flat.*

◄ *A new front end for '61 featured Grouchoesque brows.*

Early-'60s styling was still ▶
based in the late '50s. For
Plymouth, that meant tailfins
and the toilet seat in back.

their displeasure in a no-show of force at Plymouth dealers. A pity, really, because those who got past the skin-deep looks on these Plymouths found a pretty nice car.

In 1960, Plymouth looked to borrow a spark from its factory hot rod Furys, to heat up the mainstream lineup. It applied the vaunted Fury name — formerly reserved for a limited build of high performance hardtops — to their entire, top model series. Replacing the Belvedere, the full Fury family now included two- and four-door hardtops, a convertible and a four-door sedan. The engine choices were stellar, and included three that went on to become under-hood stalwarts of the '60s and '70s. Numbered among this trilogy of Mopar motor stars were the bullet-proof 225-cid Slant Six, the versatile 318 V-8 and the strong and steady big-block 383.

Torsion bar front suspension ▲ (introduced in 1957) made Chrysler products the best handling of the Big Three.

A look at the top-line ▶ Fury's interior.

Putting the Fury name on a full series produced mixed results for Plymouth. In one sense, making the series more special made one special car less so. Still, the name counted for something, as witnessed by '61's sales results. The off-the-cliff drop in Plymouth sales overall was enough to plunge Plymouth below Rambler for third place industry-wide. Despite this, Fury sales held steady, only dipping about three per cent from '60 levels.

◄ *Plymouth went mainstream with the Fury in 1960. Formerly reserved for the company's banker's hot rod, the Fury name replaced the Belvedere as the top series in the lineup.*

▼ *Shark-like tailfins were pure '50s, which, of course, was when they were designed.*

1960-61 Plymouth Fury | 25

1960 Studebaker Champ Pickup

It was the perfect excuse. What better time to update the looks of a long-in-the-tooth pickup lineup than as a follow-up to a cute new compact? Sparked by their new Larks in 1959, Studebaker took it one step further one year later and revamped its aging light truck line.

Assisting them in the process is the nature of how pickups are put together. A pickup truck is generally made of two pieces — a cab section up front for people, mated to a box in back for cargo. So, Studebaker could essentially take a new styled Lark body, saw off everything south of the front seat, mount it on a truck chassis and the job would be half done. In the interest of economizing, a new bed wasn't created for the back. Rather, the fresh cab was mated to a stale but serviceable box with bulgy fenders — one that had been in use in South Bend since the postwar period. The Lark's style translated neatly to the Champ with a few minor tweaks; four crossbars replaced the finer mesh found inside the Lark grille and a beefier bumper was fitted that was more suitable to a truck's hard knocks existence.

▲ *This side view shows how pickups lend themselves to Lark-like transformations. Cab-plus-box construction makes it easy to redo the former and connect it to the latter.*

◄ *The Lark's looks translated smartly to this light truck application.*

The 1960 Champ's front end ▶ was all new, but the same box had been on the back end of Studebaker pickups since 1949.

AMERICA'S LOWEST PRICED PICKUP—BAR NONE!

BRAND NEW **Champ** BY STUDEBAKER

handy, husky-built beauty—
yours for thrift and rugged duty

The newest American truck on the road today is also the lowest priced! And not only will the new Champ by Studebaker save you money when you buy it, but you can *expect to save one dollar out of every ten you've usually spent on gas and maintenance!*

Coming from Studebaker-Packard, these handy ½ ton and ¾ ton pickups (5,000, 5,200 and 7,000 lbs. G.V.W.) are built to sturdy "big truck" specifications. They're severe service work vehicles from power plant to payload.

Yet the trim and fresh new Champ is as *handsome looking* as it is husky. Inside that smart new cab it's as roomy and comfortable as a passenger car, with the same kind of visibility all around. And it *handles* as sweetly as a passenger car!

You'll be mighty proud to take the wheel of this husky, handsome Champ. See your Studebaker dealer and get the keys for a trial ride. Feel the deep comfort—look underneath at the solid construction—check the Champ's many money-saving features!

Studebaker-Packard Corp., South Bend 27, Indiana.

FEATURES OF THE NEW "CHAMP"

Body Styles: Pickup box, Platform or Stake body.
Engines: 90 hp Six, 118 hp Six; 180 hp V-8, or 210 hp V-8. All have high torque at low rpm, all use regular-grade gas only, and all have earned an honest reputation for high gas mileage, dependable service, and long life.
Transmissions: 3-speed, Overdrive or 4-speed, with stick shift; or Automatic. Wide choice of rear axle ratios.
Cabs: Standard or deluxe, with deluxe trim. Full-width sliding rear window can be opened for maximum ventilation . . . provides full visibility. Bonus-value features are window vents, insulated roof, long-wearing vinyl upholstery over foam rubber, safety steering wheel, and more. Wonderful roominess and comfort!

the new Champ by Studebaker

"it's tougher than the job"

As with Lark, Studebaker pitched the Champ as an economy model. Period ads boasted that it was America's lowest-priced truck (starting at $1,875) and also touted that it was cheap to keep. The standard engine was Studie's L-head six, offered in base, 90-hp issue or optional 118-hp trim. V-8 models started with Studebaker's 259-cid motor, making 180 hp (in standard, 2v trim) or 195 (heavy duty, 4v). A "three on the tree" shifter was standard, with overdrive, four-speed and automatic transmissions optional.

The Champ was offered in standard or deluxe trim. Outside, that meant the difference between painted

Studebaker touted the Champ's "passenger car comfort", but even so, interiors on early-1960s trucks were simple, straightforward and lacking in frills.

Buyers could choose a 6 or 8.5-foot box on ½-ton pickups, long box only on ¾-ton.

or plated. Deluxe models traded the standard's painted grille, gas cap, hubcaps and headlight bezels for chromed or stainless versions. Deluxe also meant fender moldings and brightwork trim on the windows. Inside, the step-up added twin visors and arm rests, padded dash, a dome light and a full–width sliding rear window.

The Champ was a handsome light truck, and a good bang for the buck. But, like many of Studebaker's late efforts, it was swimming upstream. Production delays and a steel strike pushed introduction back into mid-model year 1960. And, while the company lasted until 1966, the Champ was done by 1964.

In 1959, Lark had the playground nearly all to itself. The introduction of the cute compact was fortuitously timed. Its success stemmed the tide of red ink that was drowning Studebaker, and temporarily gave hope of a revival of the company's failing fortunes. But, the competition was right on Lark's tail, rolling out compact models of their own in 1960. Such was the strength of the small car market that even the infusion of new product from other players did little to stunt Studebaker sales — at first. 1959's stellar results — 131,015 — were followed by an equally brisk 127,715 in '60.

Studebaker used its sophomore season to roll out two new additions to the Lark lineup: a four-door station wagon and a two-door convertible — the latter the first ragtop from South Bend since 1952.

Things changed rapidly in 1961, however, and for the worse. The sales drop-off was severe — to 66,969 units — and on the surface, hard to explain. Though the basic design was now three years old, the little Lark was still attractive. The freshened face for '61 showed a beefier bumper and a repositioned grille logo and parking lights. The sub

New for '61, the Skybolt Six ▶ motor added power, but also, unfortunately, warranty woes.

LOOK WHAT'S NEW FOR YOU IN 1960

LOVE THAT **LARK** *BY STUDEBAKER*

➤ FIRST, for the heart-throb drive of the year, a pert, perky new convertible—only one of its kind ➤ SECOND, the new easy-entry, 4-door work'n'play wagon; shorter on the outside, with full cargo room inside ➤ NEXT, six stunning body styles—a full line from which to choose the car best suited to your particular driving needs ➤ ALSO, glowing new colors; superb, new, quality-tailored interiors; fresh new appointments ➤ And all in the car that's been PROVEN BY 750 MILLION MILES OF OWNER USE. See, drive The Lark today. Car of the year! ➤

The LARK for '60—world's first and only full line of new dimension cars—available in 2 and 4-door sedans, 2 and 4-door station wagons, sporty hardtop and exclusive convertible. Your choice of super economical Six or powerful V-8, Mobilgas Economy Run Leader.

grilles — formerly next to the headlights — were removed, replaced on some models (standard on Regals, optional elsewhere) by quad headlights. Mechanically, a more powerful V-8 was offered, with 195 hp and a 4v carburetor. More significant was the all-new straight six. While the overhead valve design "Skybolt Six" produced a sizeable, 24 percent increase in horsepower (to 112), the newborn motor suffered from teething problems. Cracked cylinder heads plagued the new engine, and warranty repairs dug into profits.

▲ The cute compact kept its good looks for '61, but sales plummeted to 66,969. Buyers, it seems, are a fickle lot, and the Lark was now three years old.

◄ The convertible interior for 1961. The ragtop model was introduced to the lineup in the Lark's sophomore season.

But, the '61 Lark was being chased not only by new (and better financed) competition, it also had to contend with salesroom stage whispers about the company's dire economic straits. The rumors proved true soon enough, but Studebaker still had one rally left. Sales would spike again in 1962, providing the company with its last yearly profit.

▲ *Deft styling of first-generation Larks was notable for its squared lines, curling at the corners like a stick of melted butter.*

◄ *The Big Three all joined Studebaker in the compact segment in 1960, through there was no impact on sales until the following year.*

1961 **DeSoto**

I was a squeeze play that did it in. When big brother Imperial moved out of the house in 1955 to establish itself as a separate marque, it set in motion a process that would eventually lead to DeSoto's demise.

First, the siblings scrambled to divide up the vacant room. Dodge and Chrysler expanded their ranges upward and downward, respectively, effectively bridging the gap between them. The move pinched DeSoto, and the process got rapidly worse as the decade wore on. Following on the heels of across-

▲ *DeSoto hardtops were rarely seen — then or now. Just 911 were built, along with 2,123 four doors.*

◄ *The DeSoto's dual grille was memorable, if not beautiful.*

the-board sales success in 1957 (the last, best year for DeSoto) came a ravaging recession in '58 that hit the mid-priced market especially hard. It was a body blow that DeSoto would never really recover from. In 1957, the lineup had numbered 17 models, stretched over four series. By 1960, it was trimmed to two – Fireflite and Adventurer. The former was powered by a 295-hp/361-cid V-8, and the latter had a 383-cid/305-hp V-8. They sold in meager numbers, and when the '61 models appeared, the line was further abbreviated to a pair of cars and one engine. No model names were used, and the 361 V-8 carried over in both the two- and four-door hardtop versions.

It was a sad sendoff. The '61 DeSoto rolled into the sunset wearing a face that only a mother could love. The basic body shape remained largely unchanged from '57 — winged and wedge like. By '61, tailfins like those the DeSoto was sprouting were mostly passé. But, it may not have mattered, because most people couldn't get past the face to look at the body. Up front was a dual grille set between slanted, quad headlights. The look was more homely than handsome — hardly a tonic for sagging sales of a slumping car-maker. Predictably, it sold in limited numbers: just 2,123 four-doors and 911 two-doors found buyers.

All in all, it was an unfair ending for a brand that had served Chrysler well for well more than 30 years. Ultimately, DeSoto's last production cars in 1961 would be remembered less for what they were than what the marque had once been. In passing, DeSoto became the second casualty in as many years amongst the automakers. A fellow mid-pricer with a much shorter history but an equally long face — the Edsel — predeceased DeSoto in 1960.

For 1961, De Soto proudly presents a fine new car. It is a new car rich in traditional De Soto quality, fresh in the way it looks and performs. It puts into your hands the most all-around *value* in its class. The 1961 De Soto is not a former middle-price car scaled down in any way to attract the great mass of low-price car buyers. It is a car honestly designed and built for a particular kind of person who appreciates the additional roominess, the distinctive refinements and the reassuring "feel" of an automobile in De Soto's quality class. It offers all of these things, in superior measure, at a price you will find surprisingly low. Surely, the 1961 De Soto has much to offer *you*. Below you will find some of the reasons you should look into this new car this week. Your Plymouth-De Soto dealer will gladly show you many, many more.

Besides the beauty, De Soto gives you so many *other* reasons to want to own it. A solid, welded one-piece Unibody that vanquishes squeaks and rattles. Torsion-Aire Ride that skims you along the road. A powerful engine that puts out at high efficiency on regular gas. A smooth push-button automatic transmission.* An alternator electrical system that charges the battery even at idle. A seat that adjusts six ways to cradle *you*. And all at a price that is surprisingly modest. See your Plymouth-De Soto dealer this week!

Optional, extra cost

1961 DE SOTO

ITS QUALITY SETS IT APART, ITS PRICE KEEPS IT WITHIN YOUR REACH

◄ America's fascination with space surfaced in auto designs in the '50s and still held sway in early '60s Chrysler products.

1961
Lincoln Continental

Cooking and cars have nothing in common. At least, that's the conclusion we can draw based on the 1961 Lincoln Continental. We've all heard the phrase, "Too many cooks spoil the broth." But, the '61 Lincoln, one of the finest cars built in the 1960s, was the product of a collaboration of seven designers. "Design by committee" a positive thing? Judged by this Lincoln, you'd have to say yes.

The car that became a Lincoln started out as a Ford. As the design process evolved, the style of the concept car was judged too formal for the third generation of the sporty Thunderbird, but just right for the elegantly continental Continental. The beauty of the Lincoln is in its square-shouldered symmetry and design simplicity. Seen side on, the Lincoln shows balanced proportions, with suicide doors centered along slab sides. The refined grille up front is balanced by a matching back grille between the tail lamps. There are no bad angles.

Two body styles were offered: four-door sedan and convertible. Lincoln thus became the first manufacturer in 10 years to produce a four-portal ragtop (and the last since). The car's complex, convertible top mechanism was related to that used

▲ *Seven designers collaborated on the timeless shape of the 1961 Lincoln.*

◀ *One reason why 1960s Continentals are considered among the best of all postwar designs is balance. Beautifully proportioned, the car has no bad angles.*

A styling study originally ▲
envisioned for the third-
generation Thunderbird
was redirected to Lincoln
and became the basis
of the stunning '61
Continental.

in Ford's retractable hardtop cars of the late '50s. But, while the elaborate top apparatus gave some '50s Skyliner owners heartburn, it's likely that few Lincoln owners lost any sleep over their cars. Build quality on these Lincolns was exceedingly high. Cars were thoroughly tested pre-delivery. For example, each engine was run for the equivalent of three hours at 98 mph, then torn down, inspected and reassembled. In all, a new Continental had to meet some 200 quality control standards before it was approved. And, as evidence of Lincoln's confidence, the company backed up its cars with a two-year/24,000-mile warranty.

On the strength of the '61 design (and the ponderous styling of its predecessors), Lincoln sales grew twofold over 1960 levels, registering 22,203 sedans and 2,857 convertibles in 1961. More importantly, it nearly doubled the distance between Lincoln and rival Imperial for second place (behind Cadillac) in the luxury car sales race. Lincoln kept the pedal to the metal throughout the decade. As a result, by the end of the 1960s, Imperial had grown smaller in Lincoln's rear view mirror than it was when the decade began.

▲ *Inside the Lincoln's suicide doors was an elegant, understated interior. Quality control in early '60s Continentals was unmatched among the Big Three.*

◄ *The back grille nicely complemented the front.*

1962 Cadillac Eldorado Biarritz

Where were you in '62? If you were home by the TV, chances are you were tuned in to "The Beverly Hillbillies," "Candid Camera" or the "Red Skelton Show." "Green Onions" by Booker T & the MG's was tops on the *Billboard* Top Ten, followed by "Duke of Earl" and "Soldier Boy." Grammys were awarded to Best New Artist Robert Goulet, and the Record of the Year was Tony Bennett's rendition of, "I Left My Heart in San Francisco." Gregory Peck earned an Oscar for Best Actor in *To Kill a Mockingbird*; Anne Bancroft was Best Actress in *The Miracle*

▲ *Cadillac's top-line convertible was rare, relative to the other resident ragtop. Eldorado Biarritz production for 1962 was 1,450, compared to 16,800 for the Series 62 convertible.*

◄ *A profile view of this '62 Eldorado shows a heroically long, sleek shape. Eldorado idealized America's concept of luxury cars in the '60s: big, posh and a little bit brash.*

Pictured here are two of the most illustrious cars in the Cadillac family. Certainly it would be difficult to imagine a more luxurious convertible than the 1962 Eldorado Biarritz. As the owner of a Biarritz, you enjoy every conceivable motor car convenience and appointment. And the distinctive trim of the Eldorado Biarritz marks you as the possessor of the industry's most magnificent limited production convertible. Equally illustrious is the Fleetwood Seventy-Five, the world's most respected motor car. Offered in two models, the Seventy-Five is America's only production nine-passenger sedan as well as the only limousine. Wherever you see people of prominence gather, the uniquely splendid Fleetwood Seventy-Five is part of the scene.

The Eldorado Biarritz

Unanimous Approval wherever highways lead

The Fleetwood Seventy-Five SEDAN AND LIMOUSINE

The rich elegance of soft leather in seven color choices, plus a Cannes cloth and leather combination, are offered in the Eldorado Biarritz. Shown above are the bucket type front seats. * The conventional type front seat is standard in this model.
*Optional at no extra cost.

The spacious interiors of the Fleetwood Seventy-Five feature luxurious cord or broadcloth upholstery. Driver's compartment is black leather, or optional fawn or gray to harmonize with the upholstery in the big rear compartment if a limousine styling is your choice.

14

15

Worker. Marilyn Monroe died at age 36. Sports fans saw the Giants both lose a championship in '62 — twice. The New York Yankees won the World Series 4-3 over the San Francisco Giants, while the New York Football Giants lost to the Green Bay Packers in the NFL title game, 16-3. In the year that Wilt Chamberlain scored a record 100 points in a single game, Bill Russell was the MVP on the NBA champion Boston Celtics.

The average cost of a new home was $18,200, and the lowest-priced Chevy stickered for $1,992. At the opposite end of the auto spectrum, a new Cadillac Eldorado Biarritz convertible retailed for $6,610. Despite stiff competition from the stately Imperial and the stunning new Lincoln Continental, Cadillac's position atop the luxury division was unchallenged. Indeed, the

160,840 Cadillacs built in model year 1962 – the company's best year to date — amounted to well over three times as many sales as all Lincolns and Imperials combined.

Early-'60s Cadillacs showed a gradual backing away from the stylistic cliff walked by the wild design '59s. Tailfins were gradually receding and would be gone entirely by the middle of the decade. You didn't have to be a fin fan to think that the '62 models like this Eldorado had an especially tidy rear view. Small fins perched above rectangular chrome taillight casings. In between, a brightwork panel stretched the width of the body. And though their bodywork was being toned down throughout the '60s, sales were going nowhere but up. Cadillac cruised through a decade-long run as America's top-selling luxury cars.

◄ Fins above and below had the rectangular taillight housing surrounded.

▼ Cadillac was the first to add tailfins (in 1948) and the last to remove them (1965). By 1962, fins were scaling back, but still managed to look handsome on this Eldorado.

▼ A sumptuous sun room: the Eldorado Biarritz interior for 1962.

1962
Chevy Corvair Monza 900
Station Wagon

S mall cars were big stuff in the early '60s. In 1960, the Big Three all arrived with new economy offerings: the Ford Falcon, Plymouth Valiant and Chevy Corvair. Of the three, the most unconventional by far was the Corvair. Here was a car that was foreign to American car buyers in more ways than one. Foreign, because of its radical, rear engine design. Foreign, because its size and shape was more suggestive of a European car than one from the bow tie guys at Chevy.

A sporty variation of the Corvair appeared as a late season addition to the lineup in 1960. Jazzed up with bucket seats, center console and floor shifter, Monza turned out to be the early bright spot in the Corvair lineup, and the sport coupe sold over 100,000 units in its first full year of availability in 1961. The number further expanded to 144,844 in 1962, when the 900 Monza series jumped from two to six models. Joining the coupe and four-door sedan were a convertible, a wagon and a pair of turbocharged two doors: Spyder models in soft and hardtop form.

One and done. Monza wagons hit the lineup in '62 and disappeared one year later.

With up to 58 cubic feet of cargo capacity in back, the Corvair wagon was highly practical.

A BATCH OF READY-TO-GO LOADING FEATURES—Lift the handy counterbalanced liftgate of the Corvair Station Wagon. You can step right up to the loading area. Load easily through the wide, wide liftgate opening. If you have more to carry, open up the up-front trunk. That's the same key you use for everything—ignition, glove box and doors, too. Single key locking is a real convenience, especially when you're loading and don't want to be fumbling with keys. And remember, with the trunk in front, the rear loading area and the four wide doors at the sides, you're always ready to load and unload easily, no matter where you park.

EASY-TO-REACH ENGINE—Routine access to the Corvair Station Wagon rear engine is made easy by the convenient service door. For less-frequent service, a hinged cargo floor cover can be lifted for quick engine maintenance. Special insulation gives a thick cover to help deaden engine heat and noise.

STATION WAGON INTERIORS—Corvair 700 (above) and Monza Station Wagon interiors come with combination pattern cloth and vinyl upholstery in striking color choices for '62. Interiors stand up to the toughest kind of wagon wear, retain their smart good looks. Monza Wagon is also available* with front bucket seats and all-vinyl trim.

*Optional at extra cost.

▲ *Production of 2,362 units made the '62 Monza station wagon the rarest of all Corvair models.*

The Monza wagon was both sporty and practical. The 900 series trim made for a dressy interior. With rear seats folded, the Corvair wagon was good for about 58 cubic feet of cargo capacity, plus an additional 10 under the front "hood." However, the public decided that while sporty and sensible both had their place, they didn't want them placed in the same vehicle. The Monza wagon was dropped after a one-year run of 2,362 units. Indeed, all wagons disappeared from the Corvair lineup post '62.

◀ *With the Monza, Chevy found that sporty sells, even when it's just sporty looking.*

▼ *The air-cooled, flat six motor drew 102 horsepower out of 145 cubic inches.*

In conservative times, different doesn't do too well. The early 1960s were, and the basic Corvair didn't. Its inability to woo traditional economy car buyers spurred Chevy to ramp up production of a conventional compact (the Chevy II) to fight with Falcon, Valiant, Lark and the Rambler American. However, Monza proved that small and sporty sells. It did well enough long enough to keep Corvair on the map for the duration of the decade. It also pointed the way that others soon followed. One of them that we'll talk about shortly was a little car named after a little horse.

Ford Thunderbird *Sport Roadster*
1962

Ford celebrated year two of generation three for Thunderbird by expanding the lineup from two to four. Joining the hardtop and convertible models were a pair of new, upscale offerings — the Landau coupe and the Sport Roadster. The Landau was a hardtop model with padded roof and up-level trim. At $4,398, it was priced just $77 more than a standard model.

At a sticker shocking $5,439, the Sport Roadster was something of a throwback: the first two seat T-Bird since Ford had pushed the last of the "Little

Birds" from the nest back in 1957. Actually, the back seats weren't gone, just hiding beneath a sweeping, fiberglass fairing. The look was further enhanced with set of Kelsey-Hayes wire wheels. Fender skirts fitted to regular Thunderbirds were jettisoned here, for reasons of fashion and function. A bigger wheel opening made for a better view of the flashy, new wire wheels, and besides, the spinner caps wouldn't fit beneath the skirts.

All '62 T-Birds got a new grille, side trim and all-in-one tail/stop/parking lights.

▲ When is a two-seater not a two-seater? When the back seats are hidden beneath a fiberglass tonneau. The sleek design of the seat covering gave the Sport Roadster plenty of curb appeal.

More Thunder for Thunderbird

Good thing these molded foam seats cup so snugly around your back—for now Thunderbird has a new power option. There's 40 more horsepower on tap, and a new catapult take-off you feel right between the shoulder blades. This is the Sports V-8, first developed for the Sports Roadster but now available at extra cost on any Thunderbird you choose. It has the major Thunderbird virtues—massive thrust wrapped in velvet smoothness, raw torque whetted to almost soundless perfection—but with a new emphasis. There's even a special transmission to match, with higher shift points, quicker up-shifts. Thus Thunderbird's polished harmony of power and silence, already unique in all the world, takes on an added brilliance and breath-taking response. If you thought Thunderbird performance was the ultimate, try this! It's Thunderbird—plus!

A PRODUCT OF Ford MOTOR COMPANY

Thunderbird
Sports Roadster

▲ *Torpedo-shaped, third-generation T-Birds were strong sellers: over 70,000 units in their first year ('61), followed by nearly 80,000 in year two. An exclusive price tag ($5,439) helped limit Sport Roadster production to just 1,427.*

Inside, the passenger compartment benefited from a standard Swing-Away steering wheel; the better to make a graceful exit from the low-slung Thunderbird. Brake capacity was beefed up, courtesy of a larger master cylinder, and things got quieter in the cabin, thanks to a new aluminized muffler and added sound insulation.

As birds go, the '62 T-Bird was on the beefy side. Weighing in at as much as 4,471 lbs. (Sport Roadster), it took a fair amount of propulsion to get airborne. Both engine choices were based on the burly, 390-cid V-8. It made 300 hp in standard trim, and buyers could also choose the optional M-Series motor. The 3-2v-equipped version added 40 horsepower for an additional $242. Despite the bulk, the three-deuce power plant could propel the T-Bird from 0 to 60 mph in about 8.5 seconds. Of the roughly 78,000 Thunderbirds produced, just 1,427 were Sport Roadsters, making a Rangoon Red beauty like this one a rare bird, indeed.

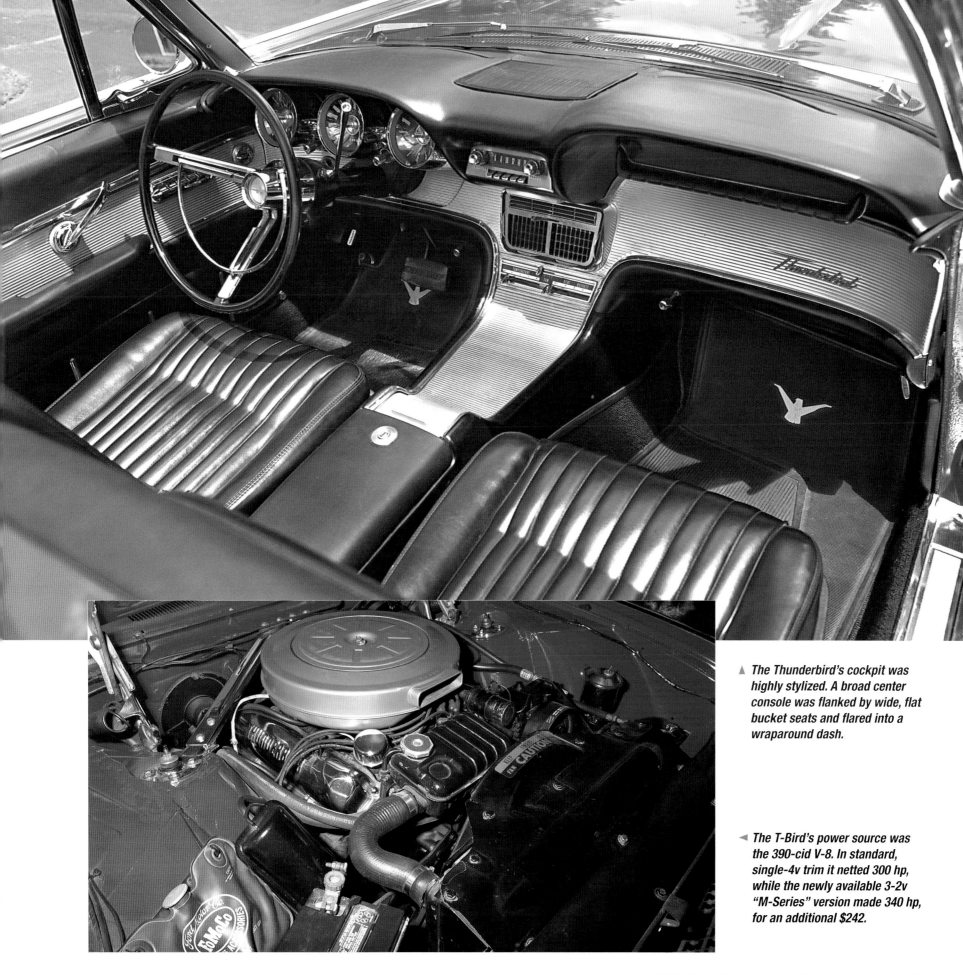

▲ The Thunderbird's cockpit was highly stylized. A broad center console was flanked by wide, flat bucket seats and flared into a wraparound dash.

◄ The T-Bird's power source was the 390-cid V-8. In standard, single-4v trim it netted 300 hp, while the newly available 3-2v "M-Series" version made 340 hp, for an additional $242.

1962 Studebaker Hawk

I n one sense, it was just rearranging the deck chairs on the Titanic. The task was to revamp the 1962 lineup of aging Hawk and Lark models for ailing Studebaker. But, the historic carmaker would itself be history within five years. At the time he took the job, though, designer Brook Stevens couldn't have known that, and his work certainly never showed it. Indeed, in the category of budget makeovers, this one ranks with the best of all time. With a combined tooling budget of a paltry $7 million, Stevens created crisp looking models that looked far more competitive than they had a right to.

The Hawk that Stevens inherited for the refresh dated from 1953. That year, Studebaker rolled out the first of their "Loewy Coupes" — a series of

▲ *A formal roofline with wide C-pillars and recessed backlight gave the Hawk a refined look.*

◄ *A shield-shaped grille was a Hawk styling staple since the first, in 1956.*

The mock grille on the deck lid ▲ balanced the front end look. It also nicely hid the ribbed panels beneath, holdovers of Hawk styling since the '50s.

THE GRAN TURISMO HAWK PHOTOGRAPHED IN ITALY. MADE IN THE U.S. BY STUDEBAKER. GOWN BY ANTONELLI

The Gran Turismo
Hawk

- *Full 120" wheelbase; Thunderbolt V-8 OHV engine; 3-speed syncromesh transmission standard. Optional floor-mounted 4-speed gear box or Automatic.*
- *Variable-rate front coil springs and anti-sway bar; asymmetrical rear springing; telescopic shock absorbers; finned-drum brakes.*
- *True Gran Turismo interiors; full five-passenger capacity; sports car type bucket seats forward, fat-down arm rest in rear, optional reclining seats.*
- *Luxury-padded safety dash, recessed instrumentation. Rich, pleated vinyl upholstery, deep pile carpet. Exquisite detail in all appointments.*
- *Suggested retail price $3095; transportation, local taxes and optional equipment additional.*

sleek, two-doors designed by Raymond Loewy's studio (and specifically, Bob Bourke). Low and sleek, the cars had a distinctly European look, free of excess chrome. The coupes had style and the style had legs, stretching (with some deft facelifts) through 1964. The Hawk series evolved from this line in 1956. The family of two-door coupes added sporty flair to the Studebaker lineup throughout the '50s. By '61, though, the public was tiring of tailfins and the collective weight of the aging design had nearly grounded the Hawk.

Enter Stevens, who conjured up a remarkably fresh look, particularly in light of his bantam budget. The 1962 Gran Turismo Hawk had minimal chrome trim and a formal roofline, with distinctly wide C-pillars. Inside, a cockpit-inspired instrument

panel canted towards the driver. Hawks were powered by Studebaker's venerable 289-cid V-8, available in 210-hp (2v) or 225-hp (4v) versions. A three-speed column mount shifter was standard, but overdrive, automatic or sporty four-speed floor shift transmissions were available optionally.

The '62 Gran Turismo Hawk was a stylistic success. A sales smash too, at least in relative terms. 1962 production numbered 8,388 units, up from '61's anemic 3,340. Hawk would last but one more year — and Studebaker a scant four. However, 40-plus years removed, we can see the cars for what they were: sleek and classy coupes, and rolling testimonials to Brook Stevens' craftsmanship.

1963 Chevy Impala SS

S porty sells. It was a lesson proved over and over again in the 1960s. The muscle car defined the decade and high-performance cars stamped the '60s as their own. The true muscle car was a mid-size car with an oversize engine in it, but automakers found that even a sporty look was enough to move more motorcars. Compacts, conceived to be cheap to keep, got caught up in the trend. Chevy and Ford sold more Corvairs and Falcons once they started pushing out versions that were faster looking, and more still when they made models that could actually go faster.

Full-size cars got the hint even earlier, though they mostly bypassed the (look fast) sizzle and stuck with the (go fast) steak. From New Year's Day 1960 'til the curtain rang down in December '69, Chevy offered muscular motors in their big

▲ *The pencil box form of early 1960s Impalas remains one of the decade's most memorable.*

◄ *The SS option package could be added with any motor, from the 140-hp Turbo Thrift six, to the newly available, race-ready, 430-hp 427.*

How to travel in luxury without really flying

The exciting new '63 Chevrolet has captured the smooth silence and effortless ease of jet flight and translated it to highway travel. Every new Chevrolet, whether it's a luxury Impala, a low-priced Bel Air or a Biscayne, now has self-adjusting brakes, a Delcotron generator to extend battery life, and the ingenious new flush-and-dry system that takes air and rain water from the cowl and rinses corrosive elements out of the rocker panels where rust usually begins. A test drive of a few miles over a variety of roads will amaze you. The suspension, with coil springs at all four wheels, treats potholes, car tracks, gravel, as though they were billiard-table smooth. The engine whisks you away from traffic lights, or steps safely out to pass slower cars without once intruding on your privacy. This '63 Chevrolet is a quality automobile, built to travel with the very best. When you're driving a Chevrolet, you don't take a back seat to *anyone!* Chevrolet Division of General Motors, Detroit 2, Michigan.

the make more people depend on

'63 Chevrolet Impala Sport Coupe

Impalas. Throughout the decade, Impala was the prototype family man's hot rod. 1960 models were the last to wear the horizontal "bat wing" tailfins that sprouted in '59. That year, no less than seven V-8 engines were available for the picking. The following year, the Super Sport option made its début. Over the course of the sixties, "SS" came to identify thousands upon thousands of Chevys that were hot performers — or at least, hot lookers, as there were many years when buyers could order the SS option package with any powertrain.

For the next three years, Chevy would spin styling variations on a classic, pencil box shape. By 1963, the full-size Chevys continued to refine their square shouldered lines, and looked particularly dashing in SS trim. Sharp-eyed observers could pick out an SS by spotting the circular badge on the flanks, the anodized aluminum body side moldings or the model specific wheel covers. Inside, SS cars had the standard recipe for all sporty cars of the decade: bucket seats, center console and floor-mounted shifter.

With a base sticker price of $2,828 for the coupe or $3,078 for the convertible, the Impala SS drove a hard bargain. Some 153,271 people drove one home from their Chevy dealers in 1963.

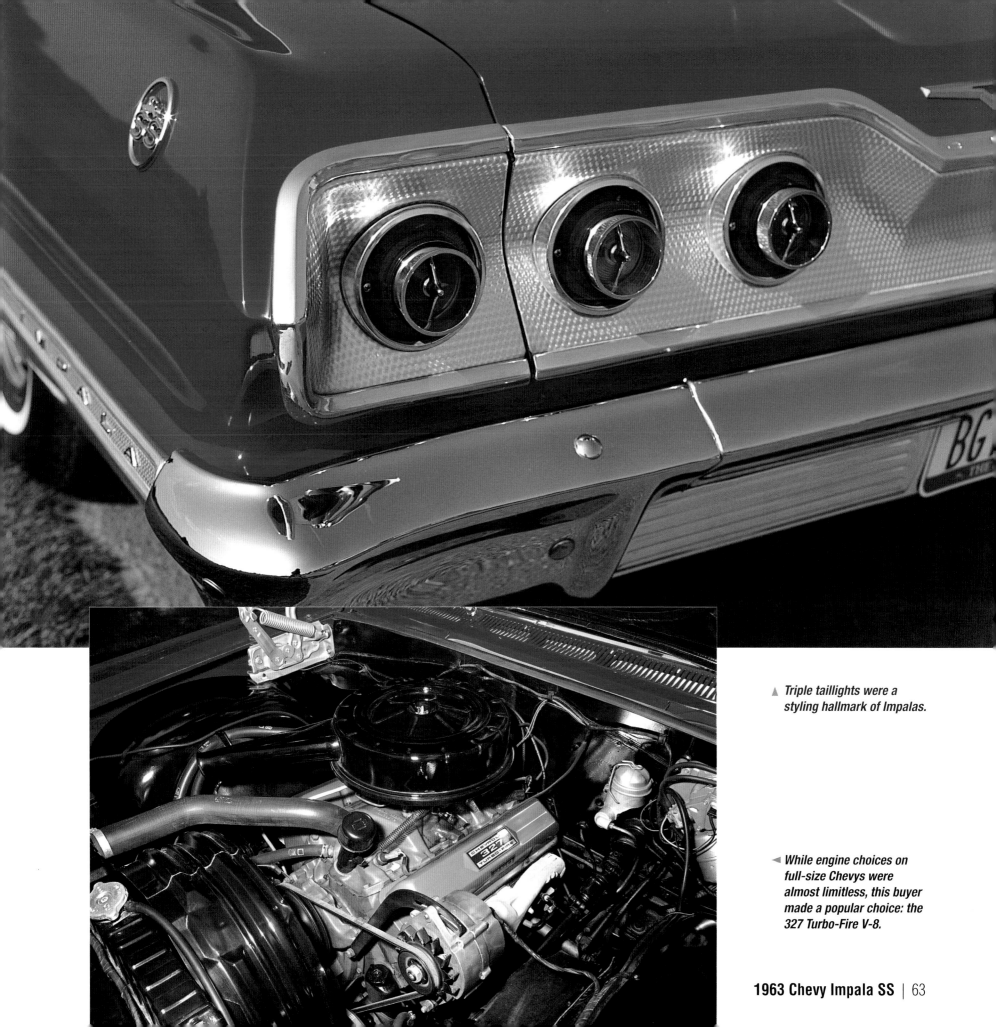

▲ *Triple taillights were a styling hallmark of Impalas.*

◄ *While engine choices on full-size Chevys were almost limitless, this buyer made a popular choice: the 327 Turbo-Fire V-8.*

1963 Chevy Impala SS | 63

1963 Ford Falcon

T here's more to life than sensible shoes. Most compact cars, of course, are sensible shoes — at least they start out that way. But, automakers know that people want to have a little fun, even when they're trying to be good. So, they subtly add some sport to the sensible.

The early '60s produced a bumper crop of economy cars. They were about as alike as chalk and cheese, but they mostly all followed the same rollout strategy. The first wave was all sensible models. Following on its heels were slightly less sensible versions for those who were just a wee bit less puritanical in their purchases. The concept worked for Lark, Corvair and the Ford Falcon.

▲ *Ford waited until Falcon's fourth year to start ramping up the fun factor. The first of the sporty Sprint series appeared in 1963. So did the first convertible models.*

◄ *The Falcon not only found success as a compact, it also spawned the most popular car of the decade. When the Ford Mustang made its debut as an early '65 model, it was rolling on a Falcon chassis.*

The rear fender contour ▶ mirrored big brother T-Bird.

Variations on a top-down theme

NEW THUNDERBIRD SPORTS ROADSTER. This new V-8 virtuoso translates long miles into big pleasure in the uniquely exciting style that only Thunderbird can offer. The handling's easy . . . the ride's like velvet. Tonneau cover lifts off to convert the Sports Roadster from 2-seater to 4-seater . . . and the slip-stream headrests are an exclusive. Also available: Thunderbird Convertible.

NEW FALCON CONVERTIBLE. More fun, less money! That's the Falcon theme for '63. Power-operated top and 170 Special Six engine are standard—a sporty 4-speed floor shift is optional. Choice of Futura Sports Convertible (below) with deep-foam bucket seats and console—or Futura Convertible with foam-padded bench seats.

PRODUCTS OF MOTOR COMPANY

America's liveliest, most care-free cars

FORD

FALCON · FAIRLANE · GALAXIE · THUNDERBIRD

Falcon arrived as part of the Big Three's small car party in 1960. It was an instant hit, selling a whopping 435,676 in its first year — more than Chevy's Corvair and Plymouth's Valiant. The first-year lineup consisted of two- and four-door sedans and a station wagon — you know, sensible compacts. 1961 was a skosh less so, as a sportier, Futura model was added. In '63, it was time for a new face and more pace. All Falcons wore a new curving, split level grille, and in this, the last year of the first generation, Ford turned up the fun factor, offering sleek new hardtops, a sportier Sprint series and the first Falcon ragtops. The Challenger 260-cid V-8 — standard in Sprint models, optional elsewhere — added some performance pizzazz to the flock, and something you couldn't find elsewhere from the Big Three. As for the convertible, it proved an immediate hit. The Futura drop top sold over 31,000 units. Only the four-door sedan found more buyers in the Futura series.

The Falcon was completely restyled for the first time in 1964. Compared to earlier models, the new look was boxier and, arguably, more boring than the previous design. By '64, however, Ford's sporty car energy was turned in different direction. Rolling out of the Ford corral at midyear was a new model. It had a Falcon platform beneath, but the body above was anything but boring. The success of the Chevy Monza and Falcon Futura had convinced Ford that the market was ripe for an even snazzier compact car. When it arrived, the Mustang proved them right, and promptly set the market on its ear.

▲ *The '63 Falcon arrived with a new face, more pace. Behind the vertical, slat grille, Falcon buyers options ranged from the 85-hp/144-cid six, to a 164-hp/260-cid V-8.*

◄ *A driver's eye view of the Falcon convertible dash. Fordomatic automatic transmission cost $163; an AM radio added $58.*

1963
Pontiac Bonneville

H igh spirited, high end. That was the GM job description for Pontiac throughout the '60s. Chevy was the everyman brand and Cadillac was strictly high line. Pontiac, Oldsmobile and Buick lingered somewhere in between, with the former often characterized by elegant performance — none more so than Bonneville, which occupied the top slot in the Pontiac lineup throughout the decade. The period ad on the following page illustrates the point: A middle-age, affluent couple, lounging on the stairs. The man's

▲ Stylish performance was Bonneville's calling card throughout the 1960s. Pontiac's top series was sporty and classy, but never stodgy.

◄ Quad headlights started to appear in the late '50s and by the early 1960s, they were commonplace across the industry. At first, stylists seemed in lockstep, and all lights were placed horizontally, side by side. Then the ranks broke, and carmakers were working with diagonal placements or vertical stacks, as on the '63 Pontiacs.

Do you need any more reasons for wanting a '63 Pontiac?
(or are the looks alone enough to sway you?)

If you're stoutheartedly resisting the urge to buy a Pontiac just because it's so handsome, feel free to get into one for purely rational reasons. Why, some perfectly amiable people hardly care what this one looks like, they're so taken with what's underneath: Wide-Track stability, a thoroughly healthy Trophy V-8, a smooth, smooth ride, even such things as self-adjusting brakes. Really, the best view of a Pontiac is from behind the wheel. So our advice is, drop in to your dealer's and try out a Pontiac. We promise you a whole trunkload of reasons for buying one then and there. (And we won't even mention that styling.) **WIDE-TRACK PONTIAC**

matching ascot and pocket square mark him as too young and dapper for Cadillac. The woman is classically beautiful (and the flower she holds just happens to be an exact color match with the ribbon in her hair). In the background, a guitarist serenades. In the foreground, a handsome Bonneville convertible basks in the sun.

Pontiac's advertising in the early Sixties was particularly artful and evocative. It was often as you see here — artwork, not photography — which gave the ad license to take liberties with reality. While the couple is realistically portrayed, the car assumes heroically broad proportions, the very definition of Wide-Track.

Subtle styling changes marked the transition from 1962 to 1963. Up front, the familiar split grille with prominent beak remained. It divided two sections of thin bar grille. Follow the lines outward, though, and you'd see that '62's vertical quad headlights were replaced by horizontal lamps in '63. Along the sides, a broad, ribbed body-side molding reached back from the headlights to mid-door.

The ad copy notes the presence of Wide-Track stability, a smooth ride and a Trophy V-8. Actually, Bonneville buyers had their choice of myriad variations on a 389-cid theme. Even higher peaks were possible, provided that you bought early in the model year. A range of 421-cid Super Duty V-8's were available throughout the lineup until GM put the corporate clamps on factory sponsored high performance in January. The hi-po ban brought about much angst amongst the car guys within GM's ranks. The resulting, ingenious workaround one year later spawned perhaps the all-time classic muscle car from Pontiac. But, that's a story for another chapter.

▲ *An abundance of dashboard gauges helped stake out Pontiac's spot in the GM pecking order. All Pontiacs had a streak of sportiness throughout the '60s.*

1963 Studebaker Avanti

Avanti was developed on a shoestring budget and a too-short time frame. The wonder, then, is that it was produced at all, much less that it turned out to be an automotive milestone.

Studebaker started with the chassis from the Lark convertible, shortened and stiffened for a high performance application. Bendix front disc brakes were fitted for maximum whoa, and a 289-cid V-8 was wedged into the platform for the go. It was offered in three levels of tune. The standard (R1) had a 3/4 cam and 4v carb and was rated at 240 hp.

▲ The Avanti's shape was so timeless that it outlived the company. Long after Studebaker was gone, a series of investors continued to buy the rights to produce limited builds of Avantis. The basic body changed little over the years, staying easy on the eyes as always.

◄ When it made its debut, the Avanti was a stunner on the street. Nothing else looked anything like it.

The business-like cabin of ▶ the '63 Avanti. Unique interior appointments included full instrumentation, a built-in roll bar and a padded dash.

AVANTI–Dramatic, Dynamic...and Docile

Avanti's promise of pleasure is clear from the moment you first see it.

Its distinctive aerodynamic wedge shape alone is an enticing invitation to an exciting new experience in road travel.

Once inside this magnificent machine, you are surrounded with a combination of luxury and safety features without equal in any other car. No other U.S. built car has a padded steel safety arch overhead to protect you and safety-cone door latches that cannot accidentally open... or an illuminated built-in Beauty Vanity. Nor caliper disc power brakes—unique in a U.S. car and safest known.

Avanti, moreover, seats four in ample roominess. What other car in its performance class does!

Indeed, here is an automobile that is uniquely dramatic, dynamic and docile. It will bring you the ultimate in driving pleasure. It is a pleasure reserved to Avanti owners alone. See it at your Studebaker dealer's.

From the advanced thinking of  **Studebaker** CORPORATION

The R2 bumped up the power rating to 290, thanks to the addition of a Paxton Supercharger. Finally, a handful were specified with the 335 hp R3 engine. Performance was stellar, and when the gearheads gathered at the Bonneville Salt Flats, records fell. Andy Granatelli's R3 posted an average speed of 168.24 mph over a 10-mile stretch. *Motor Trend* took an R3 to their local drag strip and recorded a 14.3-second run at 102 mph.

All that muscle was wrapped in a radical, fiberglass form. Credit for the Avanti's avant-garde shape goes to the Raymond Loewy design studio. Minimalist blade bumpers and round headlights highlighted the front view, which was notably lacking a conventional grille. A chrome pitchfork crowned the long hood bulge. The back shared a similar, slim-line bumper, and a broad, wraparound backlight. Seen side on, the car had a natural, low-to-high rake; a slingshot shape that suggested speed, even when standing still.

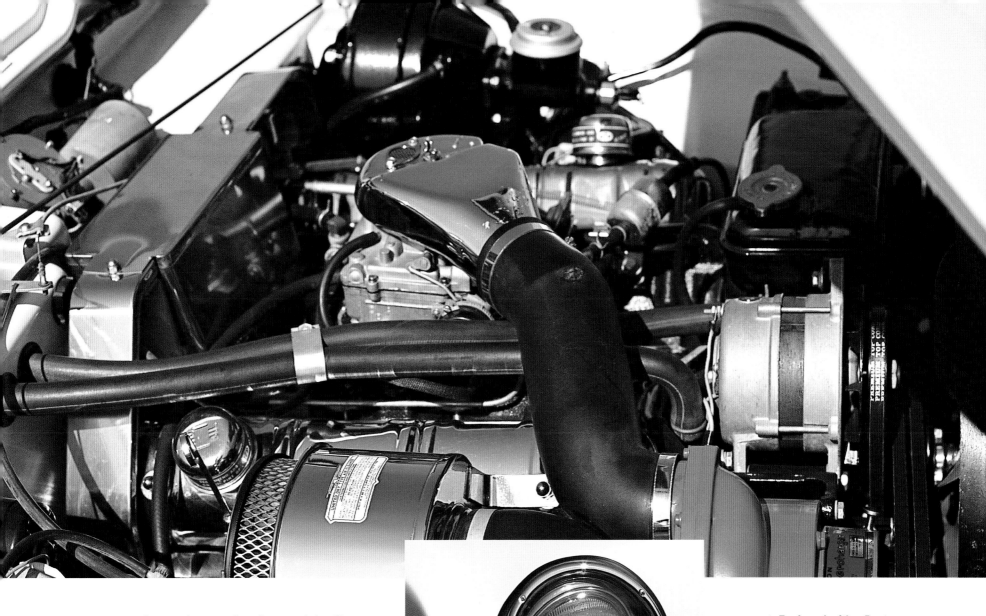

It was fine and it was fast, but model roll-out was slow, and that proved fatal for the Avanti. Production problems with the fiberglass bodies delayed model introduction. This gave buyers critical time to pause and reconsider their purchase — time to grow wary as rumors of Studebaker's fading finances grew. Equally damning was the introduction of the stunning, new Corvette. It, too, was fiberglass, fast, and sleek of form. When it came time to sign on the dotted line, many feared that South Bend was headed for a dead end, but few thought GM was going anywhere. The final numbers told the story. Studebaker sold 3,834 Avanti's in '63, while Chevy sold 21,513 Corvettes.

▲ *Equipped with a Paxton supercharger, the "R2" engine was rated at 290 horsepower.*

◄ *A crisp front end design featured a micro bumper, no grille and Orphan Annie headlights.*

1964 Plymouth Sport Fury

"Detuned" is a relative term. Compared to most motors, the 426 "Street Wedge" offered by Plymouth in 1964 was a powerful brute. With 365 hp and 475 lbs.- ft. of torque at his disposal, a driver could easily get on the illegal side of any posted speed limit. But, measured against many other engines in the Mopar repertoire, the Street Wedge seemed downright mild mannered. It was fast, but it wasn't temperamental, and could do daily driver duties without complaint.

High performance with a low-maintenance attitude made the Street Wedge the engine of choice for many Plymouth and Dodge buyers in 1964, and it was the motor picked by *Motor Trend* for a road test of the Plymouth Sport Fury in the January, 1964 issue. The car they drove was a rolling paradox. It was equipped with the 426 S, linked to the newly available four-speed manual transmission. It was also fitted with a set of 2.93 "granny gears" in the rear end, and no positraction.

A beautiful, pagoda roof line — new for '64 — likely had much to do with the spike in hardtop sales.

Buyers liked what they saw in '64. Sales of hardtop Sport Furys jumped from 11,483 in 1963 to 23,695 the following year.

The '64 Sport Furys brought ▲ back the same class and sass swagger that the first Furys had in the 1950s.

This was a bit like picking shoes for a foot race, and settling on a set of heavy-soled work boots because they'll last longer. Despite the apparently cross-purpose specifications, the Sport Fury performed well for its magazine shakedown. *Motor Trend* split the test between California's Willow Springs Race Course and various deserted desert roads. The top speed of 130 mph was achieved through gritted teeth, as the drivers contemplated the tenuous grip afforded by the four-ply rayon tires.

The Sport Fury negotiated the quarter mile in 15.2 seconds @ 96 mph — this again with "economy" rear gears. And, strange as it seems for a

▲ The 426 in "Super Sport" trim. The mighty Max Wedge made 415-425 hp.

◄ Lest the driver or any cars in the area forget, the 426 wedge came with its own hood-top calling card.

road test of a burly land bomb in an era of 30-cent-per-gallon gas, economy was a consideration in the review. Fuel mileage was dutifully noted by MT, and the Sport Fury logged an average of 13.1 mpg over 1,500 miles, much of which was driven with a heavy right foot.

Motor Trend liked the Sport Fury and so, too, did just plain folks. With its distinctive, new-for-'64 pagoda-style roofline and curving backlight, the cars cut a striking figure going down the road. Plymouth sold some 23,695 Sport Fury hardtops like this one in '64, up 106 percent over the previous year's sales.

NEW YORK
64 GTOOO
THE EMPIRE STATE

1964-69 Pontiac GTO

I t was The Grand Workaround. Tip-toeing around a GM corporate policy that frowned on high performance, Pontiac's resident gearheads had a plan. They slipped it past the sentries and into production, and in the process, they created the prototypical muscle car. By the time the bosses caught on, so had the car: the Pontiac GTO.

The concept behind the car was simple: put an oversize motor in a mid-size car and make it go fast. Introduced as an option on the 1964 Tempest LeMans, the GTO package included a 389 V-8 with heads from the 421. With a beefier cam and lifters and a 4v Carter carburetor, the setup was rated at

▲ *The first GTOs had a stealthy look consistent with their under-the-radar development. The new for '64 midsize A-body rolled on a 115-inch wheelbase.*

◄ *The face that launched a movement: the '64 Pontiac GTO.*

With Tri-Power carburetion, the 389 V-8 was rated at 360 hp in '65. ▶

Old Chinese proverb: Man who rides tiger ends up inside one.

You don't even have to ride our tigers. Just look at them and you feel yourself being inexorably drawn inside. If the lush bucket seats and carpeting don't get you, then the eager 335-hp V-8 will. The GTO also comes with 360 hp. And the Le Mans with either a 250- or 285-hp V-8, or a 140-hp six. So beware the Pontiac tigers. Once you get in one you may never get out. Or want to. (Old Pontiac proverb.)

Quick Wide-Track Tigers
Pontiac Le Mans & GTO

Pontiac Motor Division • General Motors Corporation

325 hp — 348 if you went for the Tri-Power option. Plenty of performance hardware was added to the chassis to make it all stick to the street. However, one place that it didn't last very long was in dealer showrooms. Against an estimate of 5,000 units, Pontiac sold 32,000 in year one.

Pontiac came back strong in '65 with arguably the best-looking muscle car of all time. Up front,

GTO's sales success convinced management that maybe high-performance midsize models weren't such a bad thing after all. Styling got more aggressive in '65, and the strong, clean design became a muscle car classic.

By '66, GTO had grown into its ▲ own series. Buyers liked the new, Coke-bottle shape, and bought them to the tune of 96,946 units.

stacked headlights framed a recessed, split grille. Out back, taillights were housed in a full-length chrome strip. The car had clean lines, balanced proportions and notably restrained trim. Power was up slightly (335/360) and sales more than slightly. Some 75,352 Goats rolled into American driveways.

The car became one with the culture. Songs were sung about it and the automotive press sang its praises too. By '66, GTO had graduated to its own series, and it celebrated with new styling. Departing

from the straight edge lines of 1965 models, the new GTOs had a curvier, Coke-bottle look, with the now familiar front end combination of split grille, stacked headlights and a bow tie shape. A fresh air induction option for $40 still insured 360 horsepower, but trouble was brewing. The GM go fast/guilt pendulum had begun to swing back toward the latter. The focus on options shifted to more comfort, less performance. 1967 models mirrored the '66 design with a few notable differences. The face now shone with a polished aluminum mesh grille, while the

◄ A Tri-Power setup was still available early in '66 and still rated at 360 hp, but Pontiac would pull the option off the table before the model year was over.

▲ A rear view shows the rounded fender kick-up and flying buttress roofline with recessed backlight.

back end was de-chromed. In between, a stainless rocker panel stretched north and south from end to end. Under the hood, the 389 V-8 was bored out to 400 cubic inches.

The following year brought the biggest visual change to date for GTO. The all-new '68 was one inch wider but six inches shorter than previous models. Dominating the new view was the Endura bumper. Equal parts fashion and function, the prominent proboscis gave the new Goats a

◄ The restyled interior in '66 shows added refinement and a hint of bolstering in the bucket seats.

visual focal point. It was innovative — the first bumper made of an impact-absorbing material. Beneath the curvy new sheet metal, a heavier frame housed a new four-link rear suspension designed to cut down on axle hop. Engine choices all displaced 400 cubic inches, but ranged from a two-barrel "economy" model, to Ram Air packages pushing a conservatively rated 370 horsepower. *Motor Trend* made GTO its Car of the Year, and 87,684 buyers agreed with them.

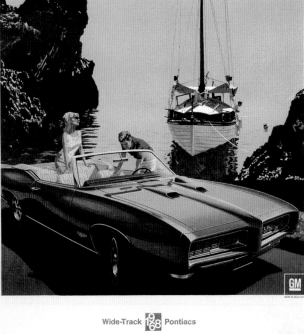

If you're searching for a machine that practices what it promises...
try Wide-Tracking in The Great One.

Understandably, the promised potential of a car commonly referred to as The Great One cannot be adequately reconstructed on paper. For how are we to pen the sensation you derive as a GTO sets off to meet the rest of the automotive world? Or the aura of quiet confidence that engulfs you like fog on a moor as Fastrak, redline tires grip interstate concrete.

Nor can we do justice in describing the qualities of a bumper that begs to be kicked to be believed. A bumper that's so revolutionary it has no peer.

And how can you fully comprehend the heart and soul of The Great One—a 400-cubic-inch V-8 that's fed through a 4-barrel carb—without actually experiencing it?

You can't. Because The Great One must be experienced to be understood. And for that, see your Pontiac dealer and ask for the recipient of Motor Trend magazine's Car of the Year award. We promise that the GTO will fulfill all your expectations. And then some.

Wide-Track 1968 Pontiacs

In retrospect, 1968 was GTO's high water mark. Sales of 72,287 the following year were certainly still strong, though they'd fall off precipitously as the decade drew to a close. Most notable in the '69 lineup was the $332 "Judge" option. Named after a character in Rowan and Martin's "Laugh-In" TV show, The Judge package included extreme colors, wild graphics and enough added thrust to back up the bold looks. High performance and high profile, the Judge was a fitting '60s sendoff for the decade's most over-the-top year.

▲ **Hurst wheels were a rarely seen option on the '68 GTO.**

1965 Buick Riviera GS

GM spent a lot of the 1960s as a counter puncher. Like the rest of autodom, it was caught flatfooted by the emergence of the Mustang, and responded with Camaro and Firebird as soon as it could field them. Another reactionary model was the Buick Riviera, built to combat the popular Ford Thunderbird. The T-Bird had switched from two- to four-seat models in 1958, and though the world lost one of the all-time-great '50s designs as a result, Ford gained a wealth of new buyers. Many found the Little Birds a little too little to justify. However, the bigger, four-place Ford virtually invented the personal luxury car segment. It turned bird watchers into buyers, as people found the new car's blend of practical and sporty spot on.

The 425-cid/360-hp V-8 on Gran Sports was capable of propelling the big Buick from 0-60 mph in 8.1 seconds.

Buick's reply arrived five years later. By the third year, GM had really hit its stride. The 1965 models are considered by many to be the best to ever wear the Riviera badge. As with Corvette and Camaro in the '60s, each year of the Riviera series got progressively better looking as the designers ditched extraneous trim. The '65 Rivs had a clean, beautiful form; at once classic and futuristic. The car had a forward swept look, with a graceful roofline and tasteful trim. The front end was a marvelous mix of mod and menace. On either side of the egg crate grille sat a pair of

stacked headlights, hidden behind retractable, clamshell closures. Meanwhile, the chrome trim pitchforks on the sides were pitched in the trash heap, and out back, taillights receded tastefully into the rear bumper.

1965 was the midway point in the decade of muscle and a good time to introduce a high-performance tier to the Riviera series. Gran Sport models were bolstered by a 425-cid V-8 pushing 360 hp, a taut suspension and a limited-slip differential. Simulated wood inside and road

wheels outside rounded off the look. The GS was capable of 0-60 times in the low eight-second range, with a terminal speed of 115.

No one ever went broke selling sporty cars with fine designs, and Buick's Riviera did indeed move briskly off the sales floor. Initial production of 40,000 units was followed by 37,658 in 1964 and 34,586 in 1965. Riviera went on to become one the longest-tenured nameplates in Buick's history, but it never got any better than this.

The Riviera with muscles on its muscles.
New Riviera Gran Sport.

There has always been a vast body of admirers who wouldn't change a hair on the normal Riviera's chest for the world. But we have discovered, lurking in the wings, a cluster of hotbloods who secretly have been yearning for a little more heat. Thus, the Riviera Gran Sport. It packs a 425-cubic inch, 360-hp, V-8 with 465 lb-ft of torque. (Numbers were never lovelier.) And we went behind the firewall, too. A limited-slip differential. Power-assisted brakes and steering. And you can specify the heavy-duty set of springs, shocks and stabilizer bar. What happens when you put everything together is the most exciting automobile to travel any road. Wouldn't you really rather have a Buick?
One of the new Gran Sports from Buick

▲ *Personal luxury cars like the Riviera and Thunderbird took a similar approach to their interiors. Bucket seats straddled a wide console, and the console flowed into a wraparound, cockpit-style dash. These cars were typically powerful and fully equipped.*

1965
Chrysler 300L

S tarting in 1955, Chrysler rolled out the first in a long line
of stylish, big brutes, all carrying the 300 name and a
different sequential letter. By 1965, a quick accounting of fingers
and toes reveals that Chrysler was up to "L" in the series. Maybe
the "L" should've stood for "Last," as it was the final edition of these
most special Chryslers. The 300 name (sans letter) had already
been applied to a series of lesser performing Chryslers since 1962,
and the 300 name would soldier on as a series name through 1971.
But, the high-performing letter cars stopped at "L."

▲ The 11th and last in the line of
Chrysler's Letter Cars appeared in 1965.
Just 440 convertibles were built, at a
price of $4,618.

For the purist—a very special Chrysler.
An exceptional automobile with all the proper credentials for hair-raising performance. Its special 413 cu.-in. V-8 boasts a high-lift cam, 4-barrel carb, unsilenced air cleaner, and dual exhausts. For all out competition: heavy-duty brakes and suspension.* A sports console nestles between big bucket seats, holds your choice of TorqueFlite automatic selector and Performance Indicator or 4-speed stick and tachometer. Now, a quick tour of the special 300-L hardware: luxuries as standard equipment include everything from power steering and power brakes to an electric clock and a carpeted trunk. In the convenience department, we run the gamut from a parking brake warning light to fender-mounted turn signal indicators. Now, sports car buffs, if that doesn't overwhelm you, turn back two pages and add on all basic Chrysler 300 equipment. Whew!   *At moderate extra cost.

Chrysler 300-L 2-Door Hardtop

They left in a tidy package. The '65 Chryslers were handsomely styled; a square shoulder design with slab sides bordered by a concave curve. Full-length, brightwork, beltline moldings with red inserts highlighted the side view. The crosshair grille up front sat between two servings of headlights under glass. Dual quad lamps peered out from behind tempered glass partitions. In between, an illuminated "L" medallion front and center reminded all of this car's place in the automotive alphabet.

Motor Trend took the 11th and last Letter Car out for an extended spin for its March '65 issue. Lost and lamented was the 2-4v, 390-hp option for the 413 wedge. The 300L's engine was a single four-barrel 413 rated at 360 hp. Motor Trend assessed the beefy (4,660 lb.) 300L's performance as "brisk." It made the trek from 0-60 mph in 8.8 seconds, with the quarter mile arriving in 17.3 seconds @ 82 mph. In 741 miles of driving, MT's staff logged an average of 10.5 mpg.

As the numbers suggest, the 300L was far from the hottest of the Letter Cars, but a solid performer for what it had evolved into by '65 — a personal luxury car. Letter Cars were never high-volume sellers, but the Gentlemen's Hot Rod nature of the 300L found favor with Chrysler cognoscenti, ringing up some 2,845 transactions, the second-highest total of the series. Good looks, a low-maintenance attitude and last of the Letter Car line status makes these cars desirable, drivable '60s collectibles.

▲ The last of the Letter Cars were transitional models—fast, classy, but closer to the standard Chrysler luxury line than some of their fearsome forebearers.

◄ The final version of Chrysler's "Elegant Brute" would accommodate five adults inside, with ample room for their luggage in back.

1965-69 Ford Mustang

It was the surprise of the '60s. A car that came out of nowhere and trampled sales predictions. It was a marketing masterpiece. A product that filled a need that buyers didn't even know they had, until they saw it. It became an American automotive icon. A car that outlasted every competitor that its success had helped create.

How popular was the Ford Mustang? Introduced at the New York World's Fair in April, 1964, it sold over 100,000 units in its first four months. By March, 1966, more than 1,000,000 had rolled out of Ford showrooms.

▲ Styled steel wheels dress up this '65 ragtop nicely. By the time they closed the books on the 1965 model year, Ford had tallied 101,945 convertible Mustang sales.

◄ An American classic: the 1965 Ford Mustang. The public got its first look at Mustang at the New York World's Fair on April 17, 1964.

◄ "Pony" interior in parchment lends a classy touch to this '66 convertible.

◄ Under the hood of this '66 is Mustang's staple, small-block V-8 — the 289.

Mustang owed its unprecedented success to styling, timing and packaging. The long hood/ short deck lines were fresh, the dimensions compact but sporty, and the look came to define a generation of two-door coupes known as "pony cars." Few buyers were aware that the first Mustangs were as much bird as horse. Underneath the jaunty coupe sheet metal, the chassis was largely borrowed from the Ford Falcon.

Mustang's looks resonated with its intended younger audience, but plenty of people with a few more miles on their odometers found the cute compact with the nice ($2,368) price hard to ignore, too. Ford's true stroke of genius was to offer a mile-long option list. With it, a buyer could personalize their purchase, according to their wants, needs and the depths of their pockets.

◄ The beauty of the Mustang from a marketing perspective was the option list. A buyer could fashion anything from a gas-sipping commuter car to a sporty, performance car, to an elegant compact convertible like this one.

▲ *Hertz bought 936 special Mustangs for use in its rental fleet in '66. Designated as Shelby GT-350Hs and painted in this black and gold livery, these muscular Mustangs rented for $17 a day and 17 cents a mile. Savvy drivers soon caught on to the "rent a racer" potential and started using the cars for short, weekend pleasure trips. That's short, as in quarter-mile. Hertz couldn't police the unauthorized use, and soon realized what a reeeally bad idea this was. The program was gone by 1967.*

A third body style joined the lineup during the '65 model year as the jazzy, 2 + 2 fastback took its place next to the hardtop and convertible Mustangs. Also making its debut that year were high-performance fastbacks tweaked by Texas racer-turned-tuner Carroll Shelby. Under Shelby's tutelage, track versions kicked 'glas and topped their class, besting Corvette and dominating the Sports Car Club of America's B-Production class from 1965-67. Meanwhile, stock, GT-350s gave Ford dealers instant "street cred."

For the first few years, Mustang had the race all to itself, but that started to change 'round about the time that the second-generation Mustang arrived, in 1967. That year, two new GM upstarts named Camaro and Firebird joined the newly competitive Plymouth Barracuda, as all pursued a share of the pony car segment.

By '67, the Mustang was still exceeding every expectation. Fortunately, designers had the wisdom to leave Mustang largely alone, focusing on refinements, not radical change.

Most prescient of the improvements was the enlargement of the engine bay to hold bigger motors, which now included the 390-cid Thunderbird Special V-8. In the wake of new rivals, Mustang sales "slumped" to 475,000. The influence of increasing competition was further felt in 1968. Mustang was as good as ever, with more optional performance models and special editions, but the pony car class now included Camaro, Firebird, Barracuda, Cougar and Javelin. Even in this diluted market, Ford sold about 300,000 Mustangs.

▲ *The first major Mustang restyling occurred in 1967. This view shows the concave back panel common to all models, and the unique, sleek roofline found on fastbacks.*

As the competition was closing in 1969, Mustang responded with a whale of a late stretch rally. The year saw the widest range of models and options that would ever wear the Mustang brand. New to the lineup were the upscale Grande and sporty Mach I. At the height of the muscle car era, Mustang buyers could choose from a dizzying array of high-performance models, including Shelby GT-350 & 500s, Boss 302 and 429s, and Mach 1's. There would be tough times ahead in the '70s and '80s, but the Mustang proved to be a survivor. Forty years later, the first pony car would be the last one left standing.

◄ *Leading the list of new models for 1969 was the stunning fastback Mach I. From its functional "Shaker" hood scoop up front, to the smooth looking "SportsRoof" in back, the Mach I had high performance written all over it. Prices started at $3,139.*

▼ *Ford spun off some unique regional models in 1968, like the California Specials. These were notchback coupes, dressed up with Shelby styling cues. Most notable was the rear view, which included faux air scoops, a fantail back panel with Cougar taillights, and model specific lettering high on the flanks.*

1966 Chevy II

T he thing about taking chances is, sometimes
you lose. Chevy took a big chance in 1960,
with its new Corvair. It wasn't risky to bring out a
compact; small cars were the rage that year, and
the Big Three all hit the beach with new entries.
But, Corvair was rear drive and radically styled for
the times and the conservative, small car segment.
Falcons were soon flying out of Ford showrooms, but
Corvairs were not. Chevy scrambled to field a more
conventional compact.

Take two was the Chevy II, which arrived in 1962.

▲ *Most Chevy II buyers were thinking economy. Some were thinking performance, like the first and current owner of this '66, one of 200 two-door sedans in the Chevy II 100 series built with the L79 327-cid/350-hp V-8.*

The only L79 faster than ▲ this one in 1966 was a Nova that belonged to renown drag racer Bill "Grumpy" Jenkins.

This Chevy II's interior was ▶ simple and to the point: bench seat, heater delete and four on the floor.

As the 1960s wore on, growing numbers of buyers were opting for sporty looking compacts; a trend soon followed by sportier acting compacts. Manufacturers were happy to oblige, and soon began offering traditional economy cars with optional equipment that was decidedly un-economical. So it was that by 1966, a Chevy II buyer could slide anything under the hood from a thrifty four cylinder to a snarly V-8. Horsepower choices ranged from 90 to 350. To be sure, most Chevy II buyers were thinking more along the lines of sensible transport (especially those opting for the entry level 100 series). But, the weight-to-power benefits of adding a not-so-small-block 327 to a small car were not lost on those

with a heavy right foot. Of the 47,000 Chevy II 100 series cars built in 1966, reportedly only 200 speed-minded souls asked Chevy to make theirs a 350-hp L79.

One such person was the first owner of this car. The original MSRP was $2,643, and judging from the choice of engine and the heater delete, the car was built with racing in mind. This deuce turned a quarter mile best of 12.01 seconds @ 115 mph, and ran strong enough, long enough to be ranked fifth in the country in NHRA "A" Stock class, in 1966. Sold in 1972, it went through six owners before returning to the garage of the original owner again 25 years later.

Plain Jane it ain't

Chevy II Nova SS Sport Coupe with eight safety features now standard, including back-up lights.

Well, that's not quite true. The price is still plain as Aunt Agatha's cast iron skillet. But the rest of the Chevy II is strictly high fashion, like this Nova SS Sport Coupe's sleek roof line, its slender Strato-bucket seats. Even the super economy 100 series has such luxury touches as padded armrests and foam cushioned front seat. Wrap this around some of the many extra features available and one of the seven engines, up to 350 horsepower, and you've got quite a package. Looking for economy? You came to the right place. Looking for Jane? She ain't here.

Chevy II - Styled The Chevrolet Way CHEVROLET

Chevrolet Division of General Motors, Detroit, Michigan

▲ *When the Corvair proved too unconventional for some compact buyers, Chevy quickly went back to the drawing board. Take two was the Chevy II, which arrived in 1962.*

1966 Dodge Charger

Cars, clothes or otherwise, styling is cyclical. The Sixties saw a resurgence of an auto design last seen in the 1940s — the fastback. A couple of trendsetters from Chevy and Ford jump-started the movement. Corvette and Mustang hit the street with sleek slant backs in 1963 and 1965, respectively. The horse was followed by a pair of fish (Barracuda and Marlin) in '65, and in 1966, Dodge weighed in with the Charger.

Based on the B-body Coronet, the Charger was arguably the smoothest style of the latter three (though in a beauty contest, all were in the rearview mirror of Corvette and Mustang). The Charger had better

◄ *The Charger's rear fender contour mirrored big brother T-Bird.*

proportions than the Marlin, whose original balance had been disrupted when the design was highjacked by corporate bean counters. The Charger's visuals really clicked at the corners. An electric shaver grille stretched from fender to fender up front, concealing the headlights. It was matched in back by a full-length light bar below, and slanting glass above.

Inside, the big coupe boasted four-place bucket seating and a full-length center console. A quartet of oversize dials greeted the driver, seen from between the rungs of the three-spoke, fake wood steering wheel. The Charger only seated four people, but it did fairly well with parcels. Rear seatbacks split and folded forward, allowing long items to slide inside, through a trunk pass-through.

Engine choices included the base 230-hp 318, and a 361 V-8 good for 265 hp. Topping the charts were a pair of Mopar all-stars from the '60s. The 383 made 325 hp, good enough to crack 8 seconds in the run from 0-60 mph. The king of the hill was the vaunted 426 Hemi, which could shave about 1.5 seconds off the 383's time.

The Charger registered solid interest in its rookie year, ringing up 37,344 units. Attention waned quickly, however. In 1967, the rear console was deleted for more seating options and the 440 was added for more speed options, but sales dropped off to 15,788. A year later, it all changed again, as the all-new '68s pegged the sales meter at 96,108. Because of the stunning success of their successors, the '66-'67 Chargers seem destined to be seen as table setters for the sleek and sporty models that followed: the second generation Chargers of 1968-70.

▲ Of the 37,344 Chargers built in '66, only a handful (468) were fitted with the prodigious, 426-cid/425-hp Hemi.

◄ Charger's insides were nearly as dramatic as its outsides. Four bucket seats straddled a full-length center console, while the driver took in a bold, four circle array of gauges. The former was revamped in '67, when the rear console disappeared in favor of a conventional bench seat.

1966
Ford Galaxie 500 7-Litre

The 7-Litre was supposed to be a 428, though it was really more like a 427. Then again, if you wanted a 427, it wasn't a 427 anyway — it was more like a 425. Got it? Let's review.

In 1966, Ford offered a one-year spin-off on the Galaxie XL. Nailing another shelf above top shelf, Ford offered the 7-Litre in both hardtop and convertible guise. We Americans are a metrically challenged lot, and it was all that and then some back in the '60s. So, it's doubtful that every Ford buyer knew that the 7-Litre name referred to the size of the engine, which translated roughly to 428 cubic inches of displacement. Actually, the 428 motor measured out to be closer to 427 cid, but Ford already had another 427 engine (which, of course, was really more of a 425). Not wishing to have the two confused, they added an inch. Simple, no?

No one who drove the two engines would confuse them, of course. The 427 was a race-bred motor, putting out 410 hp in 1-4v form, 425 with 2-4v. This motor was a track terror and powered

A continental name on an American frame. The 7-Litre name sought to link the big Ford with the perceived elegance of European culture.

The clean, handsome design of the front end featured stacked headlights framing a twin bank grille.

The standard power train was Ford's "Q" code 428, coupled to a three-speed automatic or four-speed stick. Making 345 hp and 462 lbs.-ft. of torque, the 7-Litre could turn 0-60 in the low 8-second range.

Sport and luxury mingled agreeably inside. Up front in the 7-Litre cabin, it was bucket seats, center console, wood grain dash inserts and a faux wood, sport steering wheel.

Fords to performance prominence on racecourses and roadways throughout the decade. But, it wasn't offered with creature comforts often found in big cars, like air conditioning, power steering and brakes. So, for reasons of comfort or cash, just 38 of the 11,175 7-Litres built in '66 were powered by the optional 427. Most buyers picked the 428. It was less expensive, less edgy, and more at ease powering any combination of optional equipment.

1966 marked the second year of a restyle on full-size Fords that rolled out in '65. With an upright roofline and graceful lines, it was a formal look that wore well on the upscale intending 7-Litre. Exterior cues were few; styled steel wheel covers and small 7-Litre badges outside. Inside, the interior was mostly borrowed from the Galaxie XL, with buckets and console, faux wood trim on dash and three-spoke sport steering wheel.

The 1960s saw a number of Banker's Hot Rods like the 7-Litre, though most fared better at the showroom. After one year of disappointing sales, Ford pulled the plug after the '66 model year. However, anyone who chose to give their Galaxie XL a metric makeover in '67 could still do so. Ford offered virtually the identical options in the 7-Litre Sport Package that year, for an additional $516.

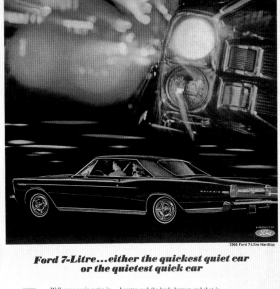

Ford 7-Litre...either the quickest quiet car or the quietest quick car

 Well, once again we've invented a new kind of car. It's not a competition car (that's why the overbore to 7 litres/428 cubic inches.) But it turns on like a competition car (after all, 462 pounds/feet of torque!) What it is is lightning without thunder. It *moves* — but it moves like mist over a millpond, smoothly, quietly, effortlessly!

It *stops*, too! Power disc brakes up front are standard. So are bucket seats. The V-8 comes in just one size, with a 4-barrel car-

buretor and the beefy bottom end that is the heritage of Ford's tremendous competition program. But the lifters are hydraulic for silence' sake and even the dual exhausts are very discreet. You get your choice of convertible or two-door hardtop, four-on-the-floor or Cruise-O-Matic . . . and just about any other added pleasure Ford makes, including air conditioning.

You'll have to decide whether it's a cool hot car or a hot cool car. But one thing you're bound to decide—there just isn't anything else like it!

FORD
AMERICA'S TOTAL PERFORMANCE CARS
MUSTANG · FALCON · FAIRLANE
FORD · THUNDERBIRD

▲ **Ford's high-class hot rod played a strictly limited engagement in the 1960s. Ford brought down the curtain after building just 11,175 units in 1966.**

1966-67 Oldsmobile 4-4-2

▲ *Low, wide and handsome, the 4-4-2 was little changed from 1966 to 1967.*

It's funny how money can change minds.

In 1964, the young Turks at Pontiac deftly defied a corporate edict against doing precisely what they wanted to do — stuff a big V-8 in an intermediate-sized body. The wrinkle was they did it indirectly, wrapping the offering in an option package on the Tempest Lemans series. Thus was born the GTO and from that spark, the muscle car era caught fire.

The louvered hood ▶
immediately distinguishes
the '67 4-4-2 from the '66.

Less well known is that the same strategy was
rolled out later the same year at Oldsmobile.
A mid-year, muscle car option package was
made available on the intermediate F-85 series.
It was called 4-4-2. The name was derived
from key ingredients mixed into it: four-speed
transmission, four-barrel carburetion and dual
exhaust.

The GTO's surprise sales success raised
eyebrows in the boardroom. Apparently, it also
raised enough capital to raze the objections of
management. By 1965, the GTO was a standalone
model, and the GTO concept was propagated

across GM's other divisions. By '66, GTO, the Buick Skylark Gran Sport, the Chevelle SS396 and Oldsmobile's 4-4-2 were all fanning out, making friends as the muscle car party began to roll. That year, the 4-4-2 — formerly an option package, now a separate model — sprouted an interesting option of its own. An available, triple two-barrel, L-69 motor (technically, a 4-6-2!) bumped horsepower from 350 to 360. So equipped, the 4-4-2 was a legitimate, low-seven-second 0-60 machine. '66 was a restyle year, and the car's hefty, handsome lines looked like a good buy at $2,604 for a coupe and $3,118 for a ragtop. Oldsmobile sold 21,997 of them.

▲ *The interior of this sweet, Spanish Red '67 houses a handful of options, including power steering, brakes, seat, antenna and Turbo-Hydramatic transmission.*

▲ *The L69 engine was one of two options offered on '66 models that featured triple 2v carburetion. Fitted with a trio of Rochester 2v's, the L69 added 10 hp to the standard output of 350, at a cost of $253.*

The '67 facelift included a louvered hood under which, at mid-year, buyers could order a W-30 package with 360 horsepower and cold-air induction. A heavy-duty suspension had been part of the 4-4-2 package since the get-go, and *Car & Driver* singled out the big Olds specifically for its cornering. Noting that the '66 model had won it's six-car "Super Car" shootout, the magazine declared the '67 even better, crowing, "The 4-4-2 is the best handling car of its type we've ever tested." The comments put the 4-4-2 in rare company. As a breed, muscle cars were all about straight line speed, and it was highly unusual to hear anyone comment about their cornering or braking ability, unless it was to complain about how little they had of either!

◀ *The 4-4-2 name was derived from the original equipment specs: 4v carb, four-speed shifter and dual exhaust.*

1967 AMC Marlin

The Marlin was fathered by another fish, named the Tarpon. The latter was a 1964 show car penned by Rambler nee AMC's Chief Stylist, Dick Teague. Based on the Rambler American compact, the Tarpon was a sporty, two-door fastback — AMC's take on the 1960s slant-back styling craze. However, if compact was cool, management decided that bigger would be better. They ordered stylist Teague to expand the planned 2 + 2 to a 3 + 3. The resulting fastback Marlin was now based on the mid-size Rambler Classic. Sadly, the short 'n sassy sport coupe style didn't stretch very well. Somewhere in the translation, the message was garbled. The design lost its balance: the nose was now too short, the roof too tall.

▲ Fastbacks were the fashion in the mid-'60s, paving the way for a sporty show car named Tarpon to evolve into a production car called Marlin.

◄ The Marlin's steeply sloping roof resolved nicely into the decklid. The emblem in the center was found on 1965-66 models and added onto this '67 by the owner.

The interior of the '67 ▶ Marlin was handsome. The seat insert fabric in this example is the owner's design, not AMC's.

**new Marlin!
swinging sports-fastback!
here's performance!
here's luxury!
here's the
roomiest!
where?
at Rambler
dealers**

Most exciting Rambler ever—and America's first man-size sports-fastback. Big, solid. Power Disc Brakes, individually adjustable reclining seats, *standard*. Sports options galore. Power? Plenty—even the might of a 327 cu.-in. V-8 option. Marlin! Newest of the Sensible Spectaculars. (Your Rambler dealer invites you to see it.) In limited production, but stepping up fast. American Motors—Dedicated to Excellence

However, there were some compensations. Though it lacked the Tarpon's zoom, the Marlin had plenty of room inside, but not in the trunk. Unfortunately, the rear seats didn't have the fold-down flexibility of competitive models, like the Plymouth Barracuda.

Marlins were offered with everything from a thrifty, six-cylinder to a 327 V-8. But, by the tire shredding standards of the '60s, hot they were not.

▲ *Management fiddled with the initial Marlin design and proportions suffered, but a 1967 restyle brought back much of the snap of the Tarpon's styling.*

◀ *The Marlin brought a fresh face to its final year. Vertical quad headlights and a split grille made for a crisp look.*

In a market where two-door coupes were expected to have high-performance capability, Marlin was a fish out of water.

The Marlin's final year, 1967, was ironically the best year of production. The pliable Marlin design was put back on the rack and stretched out to 201.5 inches. Now rolling on the Ambassador's 118-inch platform, the car's added length finally brought back some of the balance of the original Tarpon look. The

longer hood added proportion, and stacked quad headlights freshened the front end. The option sheet expanded to include up to 280 hp from the new 343-cid V-8, with a four-speed floor shifter. It was good news delivered too late. By 1967, Marlin's mediocre sales had already sealed its fate. A total of 10,237 found homes in 1965, but the number skidded to 4,547 in '66. After final year production of 2,545, Marlin would step aside in favor of another two-door: the hip, new Javelin.

ELDORADO

1967 Cadillac Eldorado

The "Cadillac Float" wasn't a fountain drink. The term was coined to capture the sensation of separation: the isolation of driver and passengers from the bumps of bruised roadways. Our taste in cars, like clothes, varies from decade to decade. The tack in recent times has been towards a sportier, driver-oriented feel in our cars — even luxury models — but not so 40 years ago. The ideal then was more of a rolling sanctuary: a large, powerful car that cushioned all within, from all without.

Different trends for different times, but in the '50s and '60s nobody did traditional luxury cars quite like Cadillac.

All of which made the 1967 Eldorado such a startler. Here was a highly drivable Caddy; an innovative, personal luxury coupe that oozed style. The Eldorado story is in part an Oldsmobile story — at least the parts you can't see. The big Cadillac was riding on the second iteration of an innovative new

▲ *The desirable, drivable Eldorado was a surprise in 1967. The cutting edge coupe contrasted sharply with the rest of the Cadillac lineup.*

◄ *Minimalist taillights were sleek, although a little small from a safety standpoint.*

An egg crate grille and ▲ hideaway headlights were part of the Eldorado's smooth and distinctive front end.

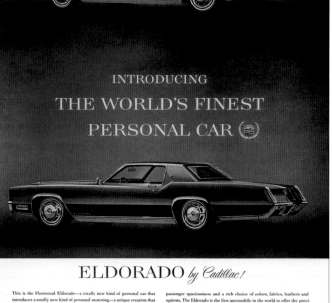

INTRODUCING

THE WORLD'S FINEST

PERSONAL CAR ⊛

ELDORADO *by Cadillac!*

This is the Fleetwood Eldorado—a totally new kind of personal car that introduces a totally new kind of personal motoring—a unique creation that combines the spirit and action of a performance car with the comfort and graciousness of a luxury car—a blend of power and poise, of elegance and excitement, of daring and distinction. Eldorado is a styling masterpiece— long, low, clean and classic. Its spectacular hood...its daring roof lines...its concealed headlights...its dramatic rear styling...are unlike anything the world has ever seen. Its interiors are luxurious, offering remarkable five-passenger spaciousness and a rich choice of colors, fabrics, leathers and options. The Eldorado is the first automobile in the world to offer the precision of front wheel drive with the disciplined maneuverability of variable ratio power steering and the balance of automatic level control. The Eldorado is breathtakingly new—but it is also completely a Cadillac in size and stature, in comfort and luxury, in safety and convenience, in quiet and quality. You owe yourself an early appraisal of this dramatic new concept in the world of luxury motor cars. Fleetwood Eldorado—the world's finest personal car.

chassis first used in the 1966 Oldsmobile Toronado. Eldorado (and Toronado) were front-wheel drive. While commonplace today, it was unheard of in the '60s, and indeed hadn't been found in an American luxury car since the 1930s. Nestled in the platform was Cadillac's 429-cid V-8; a conventional motor with an unconventional transmission. The torque converter and the gearbox were separate, mounted in different locations and linked by a chain drive and sprocket. The suspension layout was no less innovative; leaf springs combined with four shock

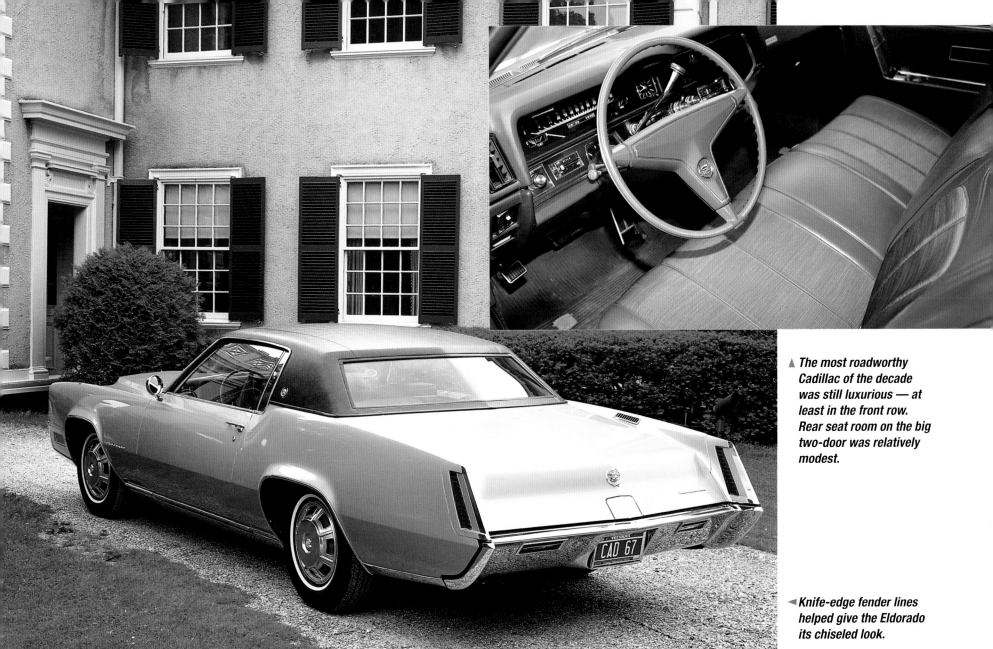

▲ *The most roadworthy Cadillac of the decade was still luxurious — at least in the front row. Rear seat room on the big two-door was relatively modest.*

◄ *Knife-edge fender lines helped give the Eldorado its chiseled look.*

absorbers in back, a torsion bar setup up front and automatic leveling throughout. Vented front wheel disc brakes were optional, and vital, to help haul down the 4,500 lb.-plus Eldo from its top-end speed. The result of the radical chassis design was good traction and, as owners would find out, a hearty appetite for front tires. Thanks to improved front/rear weight distribution, the Eldorado was light on its feet for its size and the ride was float-free, but still comfortably cushioned.

Cadillac capped it with razor sharp styling: a long hood, short deck design with knife edge fender lines and an egg crate grille that hid the headlights. The look was equal parts class and sass, and a sure-fire attention getter. The fresh new model revived an old, tired handle. The Eldorado name first appeared on Cadillac's cool 1953 flagship, but less-inspired models in recent years had tarnished its luster. The '67 brought it back in a heartbeat. It was a hit then and remains one of the most imaginative cars that the decade produced.

1967-69
Chevy Camaro &
Pontiac Firebird

With the Camaro and Firebird, it wasn't a matter of if, it was only a matter of when. GM had been considering sporty compact projects in the early 1960s before the Mustang appeared. Then, Ford's pony car burst out of the stable in 1964, trampling sales records by the score.

By the time the shock waves had passed through the industry, Mustang's population was at 1,000,000 and rising. GM picked its collective jaw off the floor and production plans for a Mustang fighter suddenly got a whooole lot more focused. The response came in 1967, the year that Chevy and Pontiac launched Camaro and Firebird.

▲ *Pricing on 1968 Camaros ranged from $2,621-$2,940. The Z28 Special Performance Package added $400.25 to the sticker of this '68, one of 7,199 built.*

◄ *Hideaway headlights are an easy way to spot a Camaro with the Rally Sport option package.*

Like the Mustang, by the late '60s, the Camaro was offered with a dizzying array of power plant possibilities, starting with the 230-cid, and capping off with four versions of the big-block 396.

Handsome hound's-tooth cloth brightens the interior on this Pace Car replica. An auxiliary gauge package and floor console are other prominent options on this pacer.

Of the two corporate cousins, Firebird was late to the party. Development of the car that became the Camaro commenced shortly after Mustang arrived. At first, Pontiac's attentions were directed elsewhere, exploring a two-seat Corvette alternative code named the XP-833. GM eventually killed that project, and by the time Pontiac rejoined the F-body program, it assumed the Camaro design with only enough time to create its own front end, taillights and trim. Fortunately, the design Pontiac inherited was a beauty. The Camaro and Firebird were two-door coupes and convertibles with chunky good looks: long hoods, short decks and minimal trim work except for the higher-profile, high-performance models.

The Camaro debuted with four 1967 models in September 1966. Hardtop and convertibles with inline 6 or V-8 power were offered initially, with prices starting at $2,466. Chevy's newest got a bit of well-timed exposure when it was picked as Pace Car for the Indianapolis 500 race in May, 1967. In addition to the four track cars built for the event, Chevy produced 100 pace car replicas for various pre-race PR functions. Camaro also mirrored Mustang's "all you can eat" option list, and buyers had a healthy appetite. Total 1967 sales tallied 220,906 units, one reason why Mustang sales "fell" to 475,000.

▲ For the second time in three years, the Camaro was selected to pace the Indy 500 in 1969. Chevy celebrated by selling 3,675 Pace Car replica convertibles. All were SS Rally Sports in Dover White with Hugger Orange striping and orange hound's-tooth cloth seats.

First-generation Firebirds ▲
shared their basic body style
with Camaro, but the front end
was pure Pontiac. Split grille
styling and a prominent beak
were Pontiac calling cards
throughout the decade.

Pontiac Motor Division

**If our new Firebird 400 is too much car for you,
try our new Firebird HO,
Firebird Sprint,
Firebird 326,
and Firebird. In that order.**

Taking on a Firebird 400 is awe-inspiring even if you're prepared for what happens when you connect 400 chromed cubic inches to a heavy-duty 3-speed and couch it in special suspension.

(You can even order wide- or close-ratio 4-speed, 3-speed Turbo Hydra-Matic and Ram Air!)

So we designed the Firebird HO. Our light heavyweight. Its 326 cubes lay out 285 hp in prolific abundance. Via four barrels. Dual exhausts announce its coming. A sassy sport stripe on each flank says: *It's here.*

Our Firebird Sprint is for people who've found

Europe wanting. Features: 215-hp, 4-BBL Overhead Cam Six. Split manifold. Exotic exhaust note. 3-speed floor shift. Road-hugging sports suspension. Much arrogance.

Even our cool ones speak with authority:

Firebird 326 is a regular-gas, 250-hp V-8. And Firebird is a 165-hp Overhead Cam Six—the only one without wide-ovals. All have GM's standard safety package. Now all you have to do is decide which Firebird is for you.

GM MARK OF EXCELLENCE

Pontiac's Magnificent Five are here!

Meet the masked marvel.

Meet Camaro. Masked because it carries Rally Sport equipment with hideaway headlights. A marvel because it's an SS 350: telltale domed hood, rally stripe and Camaro's biggest V8. Over 3,200 pounds of driving machine nestled between four fat red-stripe tires, an SS 350 carries the 295-horsepower 350-cubic-

inch V8. So you know it's some other kind of Camaro.

For a suspension, it has special high-rate springs—coil in front, single-leaf in back—and stiffer shocks at all four corners. And with its exceptionally wide 59" tread, we assure you an SS 350 handles the way a sporting machine should.

And for your added safety,

every Camaro—be it SS 350 or not—comes with such protective conveniences as the GM-developed energy-absorbing steering column, dual master cylinder brake system with warning light, folding front seat back latches and shoulder belt anchors. Try one on at your Chevrolet dealer's. It's a ball-and-a-half.

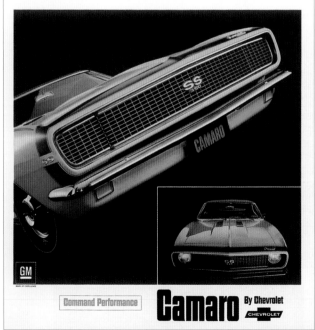

GM MARK OF EXCELLENCE

Command Performance **Camaro** By **Chevrolet** CHEVROLET

Another reason was the Pontiac Firebird, which followed Camaro to market five months later. While it looked little different from the Camaro beyond its nose and tail, the Firebird had some notable distinctions beneath the skin. First, its late arrival allowed Pontiac to benefit from some early feedback from Camaros already on the street. One such problem was axle tramp, as reported on Camaro performance models. As a result, rear traction bars were standard issue on all '67 Firebirds. Engines were also mounted further back in their chassis on Firebirds, to promote better weight distribution. Firebirds were offered in five models: a pair of six-cylinder versions and three V-8s.

The following year, the Camaro and Firebird really found their footing in the pony car market. Styling changes for both the Chevy and the Pontiac were minor (the presence of side marker lights and the absence of side vent windows are the easiest way to tell a '68 from a '67), but GM began to flex its mechanical muscles by beefing up the number and the strength of high-performance options. Power ratings rose across the board, with Chevy topping off at 399-cid and 375 hp, while Pontiac peaked at 400 cubic inches and 335 hp. To further combat wheel hop, rear shock absorbers were staggered (one mounted ahead of the axle, one behind) and multi-leaf springs were added to bigger V-8s. Camaro sales crested 235,000; Pontiac 107,000.

▲ *A view that more than a few drivers experienced in 1969 — the rear end of the Z/28.*

▲ *The Z28's snarly, small-block 302 was rated conservatively at 290 hp.*

A fine facelift in the final year of their first generation yielded what many consider to be the best-looking Camaros ever. Chevy reprised its role as Indy Pace Car in '69, and capitalized by selling 3,675 replicas. Aided in part by an extended model year run (1970 models made a delayed début due to an autoworker's strike), the Camaro posted over 243,000 sales. The Firebird followed suit with production of over 87,000 units. Interest perked up with the addition of the new Trans Am, a late model year option package available on the Firebird 400.

Though they spotted the Mustang 2 1/2 years in the race, by decade's end, the Camaro and Firebird had firmly established themselves as premiere pony cars. They developed loyal followings and went head to head with Mustang for decades to follow, before GM inexplicably pulled the plug on them in 2002.

▲ *Top Firebird firepower was provided by the 330-hp 400. Pontiac built 16,960 Firebird convertibles in '68.*

◄ *The Firebird 400 grew to 330 hp in '68. A Ram Air 400 was available that bumped up the power to 335.*

1967 Dodge Power Wagon WM300

T he Power Wagon was the civilian version of a military mainstay. The 3/4-ton 4x4's were direct descendants of some half-million trucks that Dodge built for military use during World War II. When the country returned to peacetime, the veterans resumed their working lives back in the states. Dodge sent this truck right along with them, reasoning that the same virtues that had served so well in times of war — versatility and rugged reliability — would also click in the civilian market.

▲ *The Power Wagon soldiered on for many years because of its versatility and reliability. Straightforward mechanicals kept many on the road for decades.*

◄ *The highly functional form of the Power Wagon changed little over the decades. First sold in the U.S. in 1946, it remained in production through 1968; and 10 years longer in the case of export models.*

The 251-cid L-head six ▲ made 125 hp in '67 and 215 lbs.-ft. of torque.

Two-way power takeoff ▶ allowed the owner to run equipment off both ends of their Power Wagon, like this 10,000-lb. winch.

DISENGAGE WINCH WHEN NOT IN USE BY MOVING LEVER TO REAR

Dubbed the Power Wagon, the trucks went on sale in 1946. The mechanical bits were adapted from the T214 military 4x4, with styling cues from the T234 "Burma Road Truck." The design featured flat front fenders, wide running boards and high arching rear fenders. The big pickup box was 8 feet long, 4 1/2 feet wide and high-sided, at 20 inches. Cargo capacity was one ton, and a two-way power takeoff allowed the truck to be fitted with a power winch up front, and/or auxiliary equipment in back. Sturdy and straight forward, the Power Wagon found itself adapted to

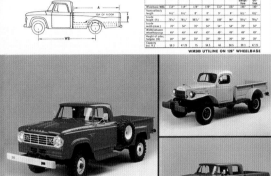

◄ In 1967, the WM300 had a sticker price of $4,295. Not much of that was spent on cabin creature comforts. A no-nonsense interior was in keeping with Power Wagon's blue-collar personality.

DODGE 4-WHEEL-DRIVE PICKUPS

Dodge was a pioneer in the development of 4-wheel-drive trucks. Back in 1934, the first Dodge 4x4's were produced for military use. During the Second World War, over half a million Dodge 4-wheel-drive military trucks were built. From this long history of engineering leadership and volume-production experience comes today's full line of Dodge trucks built for the toughest assignments on or off the road. Dodge 4x4's have the stamina to conquer rough terrain and do it economically, from the standpoint of low initial cost as well as low operating costs.

4x4 SWEPTLINE PICKUPS—W100, W200

4x4 UTILINE PICKUPS—W100, W200, W300

MILITARY TYPE—WM300

DODGE 4X4 CREW CAB PICKUPS

---

hundreds of uses everywhere from small farms to big businesses.

These large American trucks shared a similar lifespan with a small German car — the Volkswagen Beetle. Both of these function-first models soldiered on for decades with regular mechanical improvements, but minimal styling changes. Throughout the '50s the Power Wagon picked up a rolling list of upgrades, including a stronger starter, fuel pump and brakes. The electrical system was switched to 12 volts and the 230-cid, L-head six

got a power boost from greater compression. In the '60s, the 231 was enlarged to 251 cid and 125 horsepower. Heavier-capacity springs were fitted and an alternator replaced the generator.

By 1967, the year of our featured truck, the Power Wagon's run was nearly done. After production of more than 95,000 units, sales were discontinued in America after 1968. But, in a move that the Beetle would parallel in the '80s, Power Wagon continued on in other markets outside the states, selling as an export through the 1970s.

1967 Ford Country Squire

F or many families, station wagons were the car of choice in the 1960s, and Ford built them by the score. Small broods have a way of growing into larger broods, so the station wagon had to adapt to meet the need. Different manufacturers did so by different means.

Ford's innovative approach to this design problem was part seat, part door. Optional third-row seating was not unique to Ford, but the side-facing configuration that the company chose was certainly novel. Two to four kids (or a pair of really chummy adults) could hop in back for some face-to-face time. It was a seating approach that Ford pioneered in the '60s and used for the next 20 years.

▲ *The dual-action "doorgate" was a '60s design inspiration that helped power the popularity of Ford wagons for decades. The rear portal could either swing to the side, door style, or drop down like a traditional tailgate.*

◄ *In the '60s, American car buyers still liked wood on their cars — or at least the idea of wood. Almost 20 years after the last tree parts had disappeared from the sides of American autos, fake wood was still popular on high-end wagons like the Country Squire.*

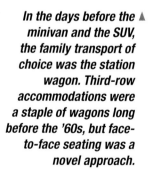

Of course, as anyone who has tried to limbo their way into the third row of a modern SUV knows, having seats is one thing, getting into them is something else again. Part two of Ford's grand plan was the development of the doorgate. While "doorgate" sounds like some sort of covert spying operation, it was really just some nice engineering. Ford designed a dual-action portal for the cargo area that could fold down, like a conventional tailgate, or swing to the side, like a door. It was a simple solution to loading people or parcels, and it sold a lot of station wagons for Ford.

Actually, Ford sold a lot of wagons, period. The '67 Ford lineup had no less than nine wagon models, of which the top shelf offering was the $3,359 Country Squire, like our featured car. The handsome styling on this big Ford was highlighted by a curious contradiction. For reasons of cost and upkeep, real wood had disappeared from the sides of Ford wagons in the early '50s. But, by then, people had grown fond of the look of lumber on their cars — especially, it seems, high-end wagons. So, for years after, Ford kept the traditional look, but substituted some non-traditional materials, like fiberglass and vinyl. In

1967, Ford reserved the faux wood look for its top line "Squires" in each series. Most popular by far were the Country Squires. Counting both two- and three-row seating models, Ford sold some 69,624 full-size, woodless woodies that year.

"In America there are 2 classes of travel—first-class and with children.

Traveling with children corresponds roughly to traveling third-class in Bulgaria.

They tell me there is nothing lower in the world than third-class Bulgarian travel."

The new Ford wagons have several features that elevate travel with children to at least second-class!

• dual facing rear seats
• 98.9 cubic feet of space
• seats for a family of ten
• new, two-way Magic Doorgate
• heavy vinyl upholstery
• optional Stereo-Tape System
• foam padding in every seat
• lockable below-floor stowage

That's the best we can do—but who else does as much?

FORD
Ford

▲ *The quintessential 1960s station wagon: the '67 Ford Country Squire.*

Mercury Cougar

The Cougar was the Mustang's younger, more refined brother. By the time that the first Cougar appeared in the marketplace in 1967, big brother Mustang had already sold more than 1,000,000 copies. As a matter of fact, Cougar's appearance coincided with the first serious launch of Mustang fighters; the GM fraternal twins named Camaro and Firebird. Mustang's debut as an early 1965 model caught the rest of the automakers flatfooted. It took two model years for them to field a serious response.

Ford didn't consider the Cougar a major threat to the Mustang. Though they shared a common platform, their philosophies were different. The Cougar worked the upscale side of the street. Bigger and more luxurious than the Mustang, Mercury's big cat offered standard V-8 power. And it had style. The Cougar's tapered shape started with the traditional pony car dimensions — long hood, short deck. The clean lines were capped by a smooth, edge-to-edge look, front and back. An electric shaver grille incorporated hideaway headlights, while the ribbed rear light bar housed distinctive, sequential blinkers.

▲ *The Cougar took the traditional, pony car profile — long hood, short deck — and stretched it at both ends. The '67 measured 190 inches long on a 111-inch wheelbase.*

◄ *Ribbed taillights with sequential blinkers highlighted the rear view of the Cougar.*

*Unlike its brother the ►
Mustang, the Cougar
was V-8 only, with buyer
choices ranging from
289-390 cid.*

*Technically, bench seat ▲
Cougars were available,
but you'd be hard pressed
to find one. Buckets and
a console-style interior
was in keeping with
the Cougar's classy yet
sporty personality.*

The Cougar's range extended from highly posh to high performance. Buyers seeking the former would gravitate to the XR7. Power hungry buyers more often opted for the GT. In '67, the engine choices included 289-, 302- and 390-cid V-8s, with stick or Merc-O-Matic transmissions.

The Mustang was the original pony car, and as the ranks filled with imitators, the competition naturally shifted to the racetrack. The Trans Am series was created as a suitable stage, and there

the cars butted heads until the end of the decade. The Cougar capped off its rookie year by joining the TA circuit. For this task, the car rode with an impressive roster of drivers (Messr's Gurney, Revson, Jones and Leslie), but even a surplus of driving talent couldn't overcome the car's realities. Compared to the competition, the Cougar was down on power and up in weight. It retired from the Trans Am circuit after its first year. Mercury celebrated the brief racing link by offering a special Dan Gurney edition Cougar, starting in 1967. The

package was more fashion than function, and included Turbine wheel covers, 70 series Wide Oval whitewalls and a Dan Gurney signature decal. Under the hood, the 289 V-8 was spiffed up with a chrome, engine dress-up kit.

▲ *Though it didn't arrive until two-plus years after the Mustang, the Cougar seemed like Mustang's cool, older brother who was away at college.*

◀ *The Cougar didn't fare well on the Trans Am racing circuit, but team member Dan Gurney was an American racing icon. Mercury linked Gurney's good name to a special edition Cougar.*

1967 Plymouth GTX

Q: Name three new releases for 1967.

A: Music: The Beatles' *Sgt. Pepper's Lonely Hearts Club Band*

Movies: *The Graduate*

Muscle Cars: The Plymouth GTX

Since this a car book, we'll talk about the last one. 1967 was a chaotic period in America, to be sure. But, in the microcosm of our society that dealt with cars, these were fine times. For would-be buyers with money in their pockets and a need for speed, life was good. The year 1967 was year one for the GTX, one of Plymouth's first, mainstream, mass-production, muscle machines.

Based on the Belvedere, B-body midsize, the GTX was an upscale performance car. For proof, one had to look no farther than under the hood, where the standard motor was the 440 Super Commando linked to the stout TorqueFlite

▲ *The GTX benefited from a beefed-up suspension that made it one of the best-handling of an admittedly underachieving class of muscle cars.*

◄ *The Belvedere-based GTX was designed as an upscale muscle car. New front and rear end treatments, non-functional hood scoops and a "pit-stop" gas filler cap set it apart from other B-body Mopars.*

1967 Plymouth GTX | 151

Decisions, decisions. GTX▶ buyers chose between the standard 440 Super Commando (shown) and the optional, 426 Hemi. Chrysler warranteed the former for 5 years/50,000 miles and the latter for 1 year/12,000 miles, suggesting that they felt the Hemis were likely to receive more abuse.

Though it loved the GTX, ▼ "Car & Driver" was less enthusiastic about the interior. In its December, '67 road test, the magazine called the cabin, "uninspired."

automatic transmission. The Mopar boys took the base, 350-hp 440 and hot-rodded it with a higher-lift cam with longer duration, bigger valves with stiffer springs, and a low-restriction dual exhaust system. The engine massage brought 375 horsepower to bear, along with a pavement peeling 480 lbs.-ft. of torque. The chassis was beefed up to handle the power surge, (*Car Life* gushed, "One of the best handling sedan chassis we have ever driven") though sadly, the brakes were not, unless you specified the optional front disc binders.

The results were predictably quick. *Car Life* clicked off a 0-60 run in 6.6 seconds, and turned the quarter mile in 15.2 seconds @ 97 mph. If you wanted to shave another second or so off those times, Chrysler offered the 426 Hemi as an option, laughably underrated at 425 hp.

The GTX was nicely appointed and conservatively handsome, and with a sticker price of $3,178, it sold over 12,000 units in its first year. The ante was upped to over 18,000 the following year, despite the appearance of a new younger brother with a "Beep-Beep" horn. The Road Runner was a stripper muscle car whose robust sales (44,599 in '68) suggest how wide the market was at its height.

The Road Runner wasn't seen as direct competition for the GTX, rather, they were both seen as working opposite sides of the same street. Until its departure after the 1971 model year, the GTX formula continued to make fast friends. Said *Car & Driver*, "The GTX is a load of civilized performance for the money."

▲ *Pricing for the GTX started at $3,178 for the hardtop and $3,418 for the convertible.*

1968 Chevy Impala Station Wagon

Few are the Baby Boomers who didn't spend at least part of their childhood viewing life through the back seat window of a station wagon. Like the minivans that succeeded them, station wagons made their trade on flexibility. They offered the comfort and drivability of a car, with enough added room for families and their trappings.

Chevy's 1968 lineup vouched for this popularity. Full-size station wagon choices included the Caprice Estate Wagon, Impala, Bel Air and Biscayne. Mid-size models included the Chevelle Malibu, Concours Estate, Nomad and Nomad Custom. In all, over 221,000 were sold.

The Impala was available in two- or three-row models; the latter faced rearward (easier ingress/ egress and better for annoying the drivers behind you). And, lest we think that folding seats and big cargo capacity were invented by minivans or sport utes, look back in time forty years at this Chevy. The second- and third-row seats in full-size Chevy wagons folded flush, for a load floor that measured over four feet wide between the wheel wells and eight feet long — with the tailgate closed. Total cargo capacity was a whopping 106.1 cubic feet.

One way that '60s cars differ from today's models is the optional equipment. Things like air

▲ *Chevy held a comfortable margin over second-place Ford in '68 model year sales. Some 2,139,290 Chevys were produced, compared to 1,753,334 Fords.*

Options inside this '68 ► include air conditioning, AM/FM radio with 8-Track tape player, speed warning indicator, Turbo Hydra-Matic transmission and load floor carpet.

Impala engine choices ran ► the gamut from 307-427 cid. The owners of this '68 opted for the 275-hp 327.

In the days before rear ▼ window wipers were popular, air deflectors helped keep backlights clear.

conditioning were far less common then than now, and 8-track tape players certainly mark a car as a period piece. Perhaps the most curious concept was the availability of almost any powertrain in almost any model. An Impala wagon buyer in 1968 could have chosen anything from the standard, 307 V-8 with three-on-the-tree transmission, to a pair of 327s (250 or 275 hp). Not enough? How about a 396 big-block with 325 hp or a 427 "rat" motor worth 385 hp? All were possible, and all available with automatic or four-speed floor shift.

In all, Chevy sold some 221,000 wagons in 1968. The owners of this Matador Red beauty liked it so much that they've kept it ever since. Purchased in Chicago in February, 1968, it's loaded by '60s standards, with 327/275 engine, air conditioning, power steering, brakes, luggage carrier and an AM/FM radio with 8-track tape player. Though obviously well cared for, the Impala has led a full life, making countless multi-state treks over the years, and towing everything from campers to cars to a 72 passenger bus!

Impala 2-Seat Wagon.

Impala 3-Seat Wagon has roomy, adult-sized third seat that faces rear for easy entering and exiting.

Impala 3-Seat Wagon.

3

▲ *The Impala was the top-selling full-size line for Chevy in 1968, and two wagons were offered. The standard, six-passenger model stickered for $3,245, while the nine-passenger version listed for $3,358.*

1968 Imperial Crown Convertible

There was more than a little Lincoln in the Imperials built between 1964-68. The connection flowed through the pen of the designer, Elwood Engel. Engel arrived at Chrysler in 1961. Prior to this, the last line on his resumé had been logged at Ford Motor Company. There, Engel had been one of seven stylists who had collaborated on the design of the classic Lincoln Continentals of 1961-67. Stunning, slab-sided and symmetrical, these Lincolns caused more than a few doubletakes on the street. It was a design worth a second look in sheet metal, too, and it got it, courtesy of Engel.

Virgil Exner was the man responsible for the look of every Imperial since the marque split off from Chrysler to go it alone in 1955. Engel replaced Exner, and the first Chrysler

▲ *After years of trying to establish Imperial as a distinct marque, Chrysler reabsorbed them into the mainstream lineup starting in 1969.*

◄ *Chiseled lines of Elwood Engel's design wore well on Imperial throughout the 1960s.*

Air conditioning wasn't nearly as prevalent in '60s cars as today, and wasn't standard equipment even on luxurious models like the Imperial. Despite that, more than 97 percent of all Imperials had AC in '68, for an additional outlay of $493.45.

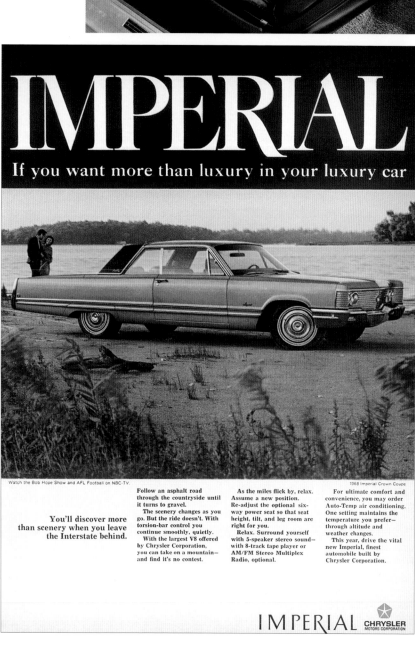

IMPERIAL

If you want more than luxury in your luxury car

Watch the Bob Hope Show and AFL Football on NBC-TV.

1968 Imperial Crown Coupe

You'll discover more than scenery when you leave the Interstate behind.

Follow an asphalt road through the countryside until it turns to gravel.

The scenery changes as you go. But the ride doesn't. With torsion-bar control you continue smoothly, quietly.

With the largest V8 offered by Chrysler Corporation, you can take on a mountain—and find it's no contest.

As the miles flick by, relax. Assume a new position. Re-adjust the optional six-way power seat so that seat height, tilt, and leg room are right for you.

Relax. Surround yourself with 5-speaker stereo sound—with 8-track tape player or AM/FM Stereo Multiplex Radio, optional.

For ultimate comfort and convenience, you may order Auto-Temp air conditioning. One setting maintains the temperature you prefer—through altitude and weather changes.

This year, drive the vital new Imperial, finest automobile built by Chrysler Corporation.

IMPERIAL · CHRYSLER MOTORS CORPORATION

products to bear the full imprint of the new man were the 1964 Imperials. When they made their debut in September 1963, the look was decidedly Lincolnesque: flat sides, upright roofline, smooth features, minimal chrome. So good were the Imperial's lines that they were allowed to age gracefully and the models were only minimally changed from 1964-66. 1967 brought big changes, but they happened beneath the skin. Unibody construction replaced the former body-on-frame approach. The styling was a slight variation on

the original; still formal, slightly more tapered. A long, serrated strip stretched across the back end, while wraparound signal lights framed the front clip. 1968 was the final year of the design cycle. The Imperial was only mildly facelifted, with federally mandated side marker lights and a deft re-do of the front grille, which now curled around the side of the car.

The Imperial was high prestige for Chrysler, but never high volume. The company's post-'68 strategy seemed resigned to the fact that it wasn't gaining enough on Lincoln or Cadillac to justify standalone styling. Starting in 1969, the Imperial would revert to sharing sheet metal with more common Chryslers. 1968, therefore, became the last year for separate marque status, and also the final time that one could order a convertible Imperial. It's a safe bet that none of the 474 people who bought one knew that they were getting a future collectible.

▲ *Imperial convertibles were high class, but never high volume. Production of 1964-68 era Imperial ragtops ranged from a peak of 922 (1964) to a low of 474 (1968).*

1968 Mercury Park Lane

The reason why station wagon bodies were once made largely from wood was the same reason that they eventually were not — money. Wood was plentiful, cheap and easy to work with back in the '30's when wagon styles first highlighted hardwoods. But, by the 40's, increasingly sophisticated designs (wagons and otherwise) called for a higher level of craftsmanship. More expensive craftsmanship. Owners were also starting to tire of the high maintenance costs associated with wood-body cars. (Think waxing your car is a drag? Consider the fun of varnishing the whole thing every year!) As a result, wood began to fall out of favor and was replaced increasingly by metal.

▲ Mercury built 1,112 Park Lane convertibles in 1968, but it's not known how many were finished with vinyl paneling. Faux wood trim on any non-wagon was exceedingly rare.

◄ Though wood-like trim was offered on numerous wagons in the '60s, Mercury expanded into new territory in 1968, offering the option on their Park Lane and Brougham hardtops.

Mercury's got it.
A "Competitive Edge" Sale.

**A competitive edge
for all kinds of people.**

Everybody's different.
So we make different cars for everybody.
Get the Mercury that's exactly right
for your pocketbook and personality now.

Mercury
Premiere Coupe.
Specially equipped,
specially priced for a
nice competitive edge.

Includes a big 390 V-8, deluxe interior
trim, wall-to-wall carpeting, and an AM radio.
(Also in a 4-door sedan.) You expect a good deal.
And you'll get it: white sidewall tires, deluxe wheel covers
with medallion, and all.

First hardtop with yacht-deck vinyl paneling.

It's the paneling made famous by our Colony Park wagon. You see it here on our
Park Lane sweptback. This paneling is tougher, longer-lasting than real wood. And
every bit as beautiful. Also available on our Park Lane convertible. At your Mercury dealer's.

**Your competitive edge
on the tee:**
Arnold Palmer Golf
Balls. 3 for $1.95.

The same quality Arnie
uses. Regularly $3.75.
Available for a limited
time at participating
Mercury dealers.

Dan Gurney Cougar.
Limited edition.
Specially priced.

With deluxe interior,
remote control mirror,
wide tread whitewalls,
Gurney decal, special turbine
wheel covers, plus concealed
headlamps, buckets, 302 V-8
engine, sequential rear turn
signals, etc. And remember we
said specially priced.

**MERCURY
LINCOLN**

The Fine Car Touch
inspired by the Continental.

MERCURY

By the early 1950s, a magnet would stick
almost anywhere, on almost any car. Woodpeckers
everywhere cursed through gritted beaks. Oddly
enough, though, while wood disappeared, woodies
did not. Throughout the 1950s and '60s, cars
(mostly wagons) continued to appear with fake
wood trim. They were usually top-line models,
and the "wood" varied from vinyl decals to plastic
or fiberglass.

Mercury mirrored its corporate cousins at Ford
by offering wood-like trim on its wagons, notably
the Colony Park. The "yacht deck" vinyl paneling
was touted as "tougher and longer lasting than
real wood." Mercury decided to expand the option
to non-wagons in 1968, making it available on its
top-line Park Lane models. The new look made its

debut at the Detroit Auto Show in January of that year. Mercury ads lauded the "simulated walnut tone paneling" not only for its looks, but also for its practicality, as a stopper of door dings. Relegating the would-be walnut to the role of a reeeally big-body side molding on the company flagship seems unnecessary. The woodie look was about fashion, not function, and it added a dash of cosmetic class to the slab sided body of the big Mercs.

A brand new Park Lane convertible cost $3,822 in 1968. While it's not known how many of the 1,112 built were ordered with yacht deck planking, the number was undoubtedly small. It became infinitely smaller the next year — like zero. The Park Lane, a staple series in the Mercury lineup since 1958, was replaced in 1969 by the Marquis.

▲ *A luxurious sunroom for six. All Mercurys were treated to a dashboard makeover in 1968.*

▲ *Park Lanes were powered by a 315-hp version of the 390 V-8.*

1968 Shelby Mustang GT 500KR

T he Mustang didn't really need a sales boost. The sporty compacts sold a staggering 680,689 in its first full model year, but in the 1960s, Ford was keen on burnishing its brand by winning some races. Mustang seemed like a smart candidate for the job, and Ford enlisted racer-turned-car-builder Carroll Shelby to throw a saddle over the popular pony cars and transform them for the track. In his Los Angeles shop, Shelby and company took Mustang fastbacks and turned them into Shelby-Mustang GT 350s. Street and GT 350R racing versions were offered for sale, the latter proving track worthy enough to dominate their class in Sports Car Club of America competition.

▲ *Shelby had produced a handful of convertibles over the years, but 1968 was the first year for a regular production ragtop. A total of 318 were built in '68 at a price of $4,594 each.*

◀ *Combined sales of 4,450 for all models in '68 was the high water mark for Shelby.*

The speedometer and ▶ tach were upsized for '68, and secondary gauges were relocated to the center console.

Buy It . . . or watch It go by

King of the Road!

Carroll Shelby has pulled the trick of the year. He's combined Ford's new *drag champion* 428 Cobra Jet engine with his *complete* road car, the Cobra GT 500. Result? Cobra GT 500-KR . . . King of the Road.

Drag champion engine? The 428 Cobra Jet grabbed Super Stock Eliminator honors at the Pomona Winternationals. It delivers 335 hp at 5400 rpm, churns up 440 lbs/ft of torque at a usable 3400. Look for 0 to 60 times that will snap your eyeballs! "Hot Rod" Magazine calls it ". . . the fastest-running Pure Stock in the history of man."

The complete Shelby Cobra GT is ready-made for the "all-there" Cobra Jet. Power is controlled by adjustable shocks, heavy-duty suspension, four-speed transmission (with automatic a low cost option), beefy driveline and torque-sensitive locking rear. All standard—along with 16-to-1 ratio power steering, high performance tires, power disc front brakes. These essentials—plus safety features, luxury interiors and limited-edition styling—are engineered-in, not just offered as options.

The game is Follow-the-Leader. The name of the game is Cobra GT 500-KR. Or play a slightly tamer game with the Cobra GT 350. But make your play at your Shelby dealer . . . today.

As the decade progressed, Shelby-Mustangs became less of the former, more of the latter. Production moved from California to Michigan, as the cars moved the meter gradually from raw towards refinement. Performance purists lamented the loss of the Shelby's roughhewn, race-ready personality. Still, marketplace realities ruled. Ford reasoned that there were far fewer buyers amongst the racers than they were amongst regular folk, and improving a car's bottom line isn't always consistent with improving its top end. So, the Shelbys grew bigger and better appointed.

▼ Cobra buyers interested in added
venom could opt for the mighty
427 side oiler.

1968 models (now known as Shelby Cobras) were
transitional models, with one foot in the garage,
and the other in the living room. Proof of the latter
popped up on the option sheet, in the form of the
newly available air conditioning.

As to the former, at mid year, the lineup's top
slot was taken over by the GT 500KR. "KR" stood
for King of the Road, and these models were most
notable for the addition of the hotter 428 Cobra Jet
engine. The performance boost of the new motor
provided some pushback against the growing

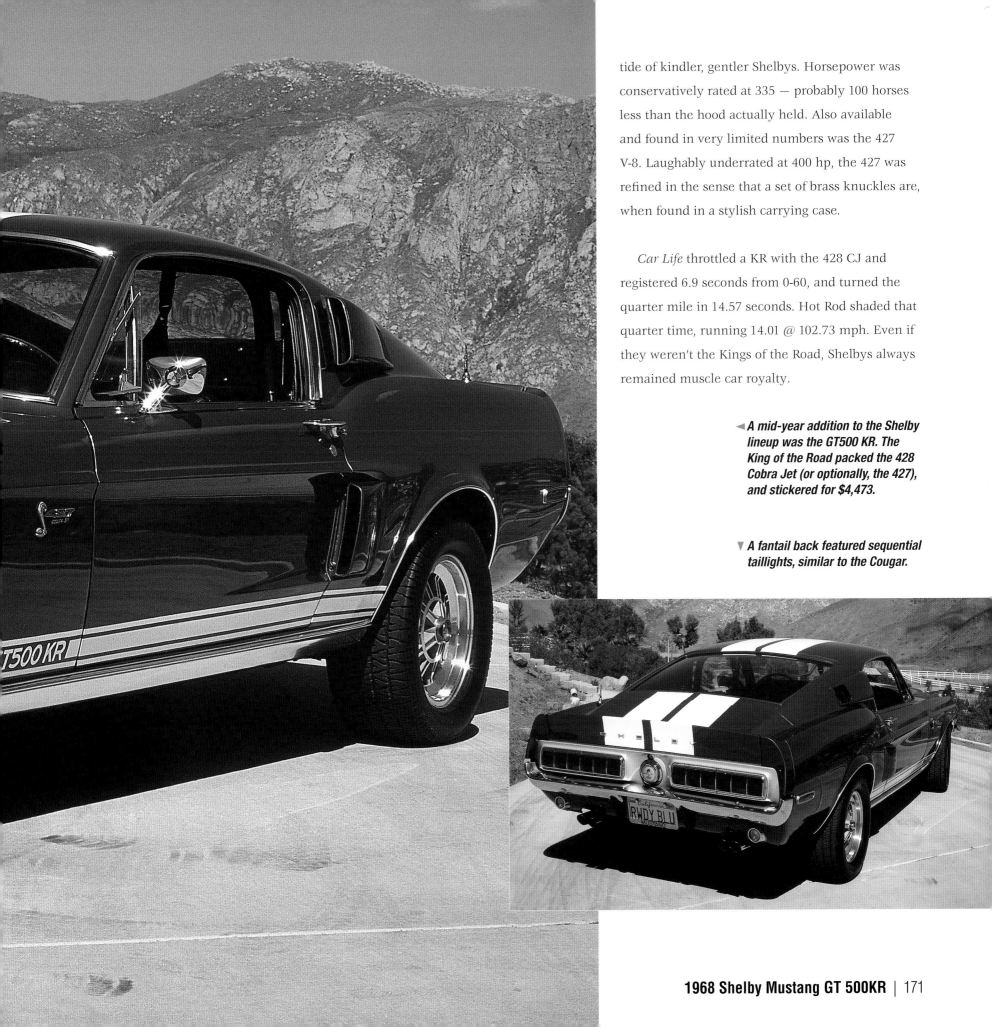

tide of kindler, gentler Shelbys. Horsepower was conservatively rated at 335 — probably 100 horses less than the hood actually held. Also available and found in very limited numbers was the 427 V-8. Laughably underrated at 400 hp, the 427 was refined in the sense that a set of brass knuckles are, when found in a stylish carrying case.

Car Life throttled a KR with the 428 CJ and registered 6.9 seconds from 0-60, and turned the quarter mile in 14.57 seconds. Hot Rod shaded that quarter time, running 14.01 @ 102.73 mph. Even if they weren't the Kings of the Road, Shelbys always remained muscle car royalty.

◄ *A mid-year addition to the Shelby lineup was the GT500 KR. The King of the Road packed the 428 Cobra Jet (or optionally, the 427), and stickered for $4,473.*

▼ *A fantail back featured sequential taillights, similar to the Cougar.*

1969
AMC SC/Rambler-Hurst

Ah, the irony. At the dawn of the 1960s, American Motors had the third-best selling car line in the industry. It got there by building frugal economy cars and wagging fingers at the excesses of Detroit's Big Three, builders of all those gas guzzlers. Then, as the decade drew to a close, there was AMC shamelessly rolling out a gas-swilling, tire-burning, eye-popping muscle car of its own. The change of heart seemed completely out of character; like a miser suddenly taking off on a Vegas spending spree. Maybe the only thing more surprising than the fact that AMC did it was the realization of how well they did it. This little Rambler could rock and roll!

▲ *Look past the patriotic paint job and you find that the SC/Rambler was based on the Rogue hardtop. The SC made its debut at the Chicago Auto Show in March 1969.*

◄ *The idea of a wild-eyed muscle car from the sensible, economy-minded folks at AMC must have struck a lot of people as strange in 1969 – one reason why the shoebox SC/Rambler hot rod sold just 1,512 units.*

The SC/Rambler's interior ▲ *was a strange mix of snappy and sedate. Charcoal vinyl bench seats were fitted with red, white and blue headrests. A big tach was strapped on the steering column, and the Hurst T- Handle shifter gave the Scrambler the look of a budget blaster — which it was.*

Partnering with Hurst Performance Inc., AMC started with a Rambler Rogue hardtop. Into this shoebox shape was poured a passel of high-performance parts, judiciously selected by the gearheads at Hurst. A 390-cid/315-hp V-8 was wedged into the engine bay and fed cold air through a wide mouth hood scoop. Hooked to the big block was a close-ratio four-speed transmission. The chassis was pumped up with heavy-duty springs, shocks and a sway bar, and backed up by a Dana 3.54 Twin Grip rear end. Mag-style wheels were shod with Goodyear Polyglas tires, and slowed by power front disc brakes. Inside, a Sun Tach sat front and

AMC must have thought that the cold, dense air that it was force-feeding into the 390 engine was exceptionally dense. The company provided an on-scoop road map, showing the air flow which way to go.

The SC/Rambler was a turn-key hot rod. AMC claimed quarter-mile times in the 14.3-second range right out of the wrapper. Buff books did even better, with "Car Life" posting a 14.14 ET.

center on the steering column, and — naturally — a Hurst T-handle shifter was close at hand.

The package was wrapped in one of two profoundly patriotic paint schemes. And if you thought the red, white and blue visuals were eye opening, so, too, was the performance. The "Scrambler" was a budget blaster: a legitimate, low-14-second quarter-mile car, right out of the wrapper. As an AMC ad put it, "With this car, you could make life miserable for any GTO, Road Runner, Cobra Jet or Mach 1." All, for $2,998.

It made heads turn and pulses quicken. But, as fast as it was, it was even quicker to depart. The Rambler SC was a one-and-done member of the '60's muscle car class, exiting after the 1969 model year with 1,512 sales.

1969 Chevy C10 Pickup

As the 1960s rolled on, trucks were increasingly big business for Chevy. Where the bow tie guys pushed some 394,000 trucks off the assembly line in 1960, the number had more than doubled in a decade's time. Almost 685,000 were built in '69.

Pickups were the backbone of the light truck market, then as now, but the market these days is markedly different. At this writing, Ford's F-Series pickup has been the best-selling vehicle, car or truck, in the country for 24 years straight, and sold over 900,000 units in each of the last two calendar years. Clearly, something about pickups resonates with American drivers. But, while we buy far more trucks than we did in the '60s, we're far less likely to use them as trucks.

Even though most worked for a living, trucks had become sophisticated enough by the late-'60s that they were comfortable for daily use. Many of Chevy's print ads for the period showed women behind the wheel; a subtle invitation for the ladies to consider the more refined world of the pickup truck.

▲ *Fleetside or Stepside? When buying a Chevy pickup, your decisions started here. The Fleetside had a conventional, slab-sided box, while Stepsides had running boards aft to aid side loading.*

The CST cabin was ▶ exceptionally handsome, as Chevy sought to blur the lines between cars and trucks. A tooled-look vinyl interior was complemented by an option list that included air conditioning, power options and bucket seats.

Five engine choices were ▲ available across Chevy's light truck line in '69, including 250 and 292-cid sixes and a trio of V-8's: 307, 396 and the popular 255-hp 350, seen here.

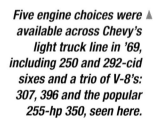

Chevy touted the ▶ durability of its double-wall cab construction. The combination of a rugged outside and refined inside made Chevy trucks "a pleasant place to work."

The '69 Chevy light truck line came in for a facelift. A large, Chevy bowtie was parked front and center on the hood. Below, round headlights were framed in square housings. Running in between, a broad, brightwork bar bisected the grille, with the Chevrolet name spelled out across its length. Fleetside and Stepside bodies were offered, and buyers had a choice of five engines, ranging from an economical six to the burly 396 V-8. New to the charts was Chevy's perennial favorite, the 350 small-block V-8. The range of gear changers included a three-speed manual, and two- or three-speed automatic.

Though many trucks still toiled through workaday lives, their owners were being offered the option of less-Spartan surroundings. Interior highlights for '69 included a standard, "low profile" steering wheel and redesigned, foot-operated parking brake. The seatback design was improved for greater comfort and buyers could step up to air conditioning or the dressy Custom Sport Truck package, with an embossed look for seats and door panels and full carpeting. It would be decades before trucks would really take off in popularity as non-working, daily drivers. But even back in '69, Chevy was exploring the boundaries between work and play.

Half-ton Fleetside CST Pickup   Half-ton Stepside Pickup

A Chevy pickup is built to be womanhandled.

Don't get us wrong. Mankind's favorite truck is as tough as ever. It's got double-wall steel in all the vital areas. More power than any other popular pickup. And a rugged frame underneath. But the '69 Chevy has womankind in mind, too. There's the smooth full coil spring ride, for example. And soft molded foam seats. Plus all the extras you can order, from power steering to air conditioning. It's enough to make the grade with any gal—or guy who works, or camps, in a truck. The '69 Chevy pickup is a lot more truck for a lot more people. As you and your spouse will agree, when you visit your Chevrolet dealer's. . . . Chevrolet Division of General Motors, Detroit, Mich.

CHEVROLET

More trucks are Chevrolets because Chevrolet is a more truck!

▲ *Chevy offered 16 Fleetside models in 1969, with the CST/10 being the dressiest half-ton.*

1969 Chevy Chevelle SS 396

I n 1969 America, mind-altering drugs were part of the landscape. And, if any American automakers could've seen into the future, they would be reaching for a sedative at the very least. Within three years, sales in the booming muscle car segment would bell bottom out; a victim of energy and insurance issues. What followed was a

mad scramble to field economy cars, as Japanese brands grabbed a toehold in the market that they would never relinquish.

But, back in '69, nobody knew, and GM's focus was on how to expand its share of the muscle car market against an ever-expanding pool of

A blackout grille and power bulge were part of the SS package.

The SS 396 reverted from full model to option package status in '69; a $348 up-charge on Malibu sport coupe, convertible or Chevelle 300 two-door sedan.

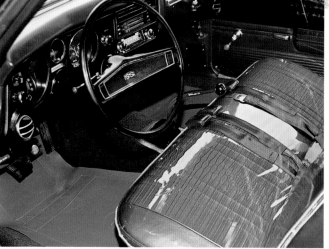

*Buckets and a console were ▶
optional, not standard, on the
SS package.*

contenders. Chevelle had found a winning formula
in 1965 with the SS 396 models and, after stopping
to pick up a hot, new body style in 1968, continued
on at warp speed. In '69, Chevy offered the SS 396
option across the Chevelle line. Hardtop, sedan
or convertible; Chevelle, Chevelle 300 or Malibu,
as long as you could peel an extra $347.60 out of
your wallet, you could stuff a big block in it. And
what a big block: in the swan song year for the 396,

the bow tie guys offered it in 325-, 350- and 375-hp versions. Savvy buyers could get a 427-cid/425-hp "Rat"-powered Chevelle using the Central Office Production Order system.

1970 saw the final expansion and peak expression of the Chevelle SS. The 396 big block was punched out one last time to 454 cubic inches. Solid lifter LS6 versions pushed a prodigious 450 hp and could trip the quarter-mile traps at a shade under 14 seconds. The expansion was followed immediately by a retraction (the hottest '71 Chevelle could muster only 365 hp), and soon after, extinction. The Chevelle series disappeared after 1973. The smoke from the final blast of the 1970 Chevelle, and its subsequent fast retreat, has almost obscured how fine the '69 SS 396 models were. Buyers knew, though, and snapped up 86,300 of them.

1969 Dodge Charger 500

NASCAR, street car. The Dodge Charger 500 was both; part of a one-two punch that Dodge threw at NASCAR in 1969. Win on the NASCAR circuit and you make money — twice. First, when you take the trophy on Sunday. Second, when the thousands that see you win walk into their neighborhood car dealer on Monday and buy one of your products. It's big money, and it's worth it — that's why the Big Three do it.

When Dodge's NASCAR fortunes were flagging in 1969, it did something about it. The company's first foray into building a faster stock car was the Charger 500. Dodge's approach was to improve the car's ability to cut through the air cleanly. These days, racers at every level consider aerodynamics, but in '69, making a car more slippery was new science. The changes looked simple enough. Up front, the recessed grille was

Second-generation Chargers were a smash hit for Dodge. The purpose-built Charger 500 was produced in intentionally low numbers, but mainline models sold strongly. Gen. 2 debut models tallied 96,108 units in 1968, followed by 89,199 in 1969.

Interior options on ▶ this '69 include power steering, power brakes, AM/8-track and a sport steering wheel.

The backlight was ▶ raised to the same level as the sail panels.

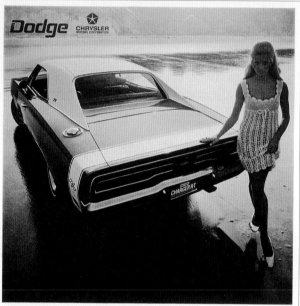

Charger 500s are rare. ▲ Hemi cars are rare. So, how rare is a Charger 500 Hemi car? Some estimates put the number of '69 Charger 500s outfitted with the 426 (like this one) at no more than 35.

pulled flush with the front end. In back, the rear glass was raised even with the top of the sail panels. The results weren't as handsome as the regular issue Charger, but this was about function, not fashion, and the results on the racetrack were very good. With more down force on both ends, the Charger 500 was faster, and the NASCAR entries started winning a lot of races.

New technology has a very short shelf life, though, and the Charger 500's aero-gains weren't lost on the competition. Ford took one too many looks at the back end of a Charger 500 and retreated to the wind tunnel. It promptly returned with the Torino Talladega and the Cyclone Spoiler II, raising the stakes again. Chrysler upped the ante one more time that year with the amazingly aerodynamic Dodge

Charger Daytona, followed later by the Plymouth Road Runner Superbird — cars so successful that NACSAR banned them by 1971.

To play by NASCAR's rules, an automaker had to produce at least 500 street versions of any car that they wanted to race. Dodge dutifully "homologated" 500 Chargers. Or did they? The actual number built is most often pegged at 392, and it's entirely possible that with all eyes on the race track, nobody much was keeping track of just how many copies hit the street. The low build count and its status as an aerodynamic pioneer will always assure the Charger 500 a place at the table of the '60s' most coveted cars.

▲ *Go with the flow. The Charger 500 pioneered in the field of auto aerodynamics. The function-first, fashion-after approach was unique for its time.*

1969 Plymouth Barracuda Mod Top

F ashion happens in a flash. Car design cycles are far slower. Styles seen on a Paris runway can be bought in a New York City shop in a matter of months. But, changes in sheet metal are more often measured in years. For that reason, annual face lifts are the automaker's way to keep current with trends, while marking time 'til the next, full redesign. For the most part, these "freshenings" are straightforward affairs: a revamped grille, tweaked taillights, maybe some updated wheels and a few new hues on the color chart. But, when the times themselves are more colorful, so too, are the efforts to keep pace with them. In the latter category,

we submit the following example, for your consideration: the Mod Top.

If you aren't old enough to have lived through them, the late-'60s in America were wild times in many ways. The clothes and hair of many young folks mirrored the times they lived in: radical, casual and colorful. Automakers looking to tie in their annual auto facelifts to these tie-dyed times had a tall order to fill. While I'd wager that the idea of a buckskin fringe top at least crossed the minds of some would-be stylist, it (thankfully) never came to pass. What did make it into

▲ *This Sunfire Yellow Barracuda was one of 12,757 coupes built in '69.*

◄ *1969 was the third and last year of Barracuda's second generation. It was also the last time that the lineup had three body styles. When the car was restyled for 1970, notchback coupe and convertible models returned, but not the fastback.*

Mod Tops were most ▲
commonly paired with
matching floral interiors.

production, though, was something almost as wild, and as recognizably "'60s" as a peace sign. In the days of flower power, Chrysler Corporation offered flowered, pop print vinyl tops.

Mod tops were available only on select hardtop models (Dart, Coronet, Superbee, Satellite and Barracuda), and only in 1969-70. The most commonly seen combinations (though by no means common) were a neon looking, blue-green floral pattern on the Plymouth Satellite, and a yellow and black combo offered on Barracudas. Published sources suggest that less than 3,000 total cars were fitted with a floral fedora.

Barracuda buyers could opt for the further, budding indulgence of a matching interior, or just do the cabin with a standard vinyl top. Though flower power was a unisex phenomenon, Plymouth print ads were clearly pitched at women. An ad for the '69 Mod Top Barracuda touted le chapeau fleuri, while reminding readers

Introducing the car you wear.

The 1969 Barracuda with Pop Prints.
Look what Plymouth's up to now. Pop prints, mod tops. You name it. Even if you can't name it, you can have it.

A floral vinyl top. Or floral seat and interior trim. Or both. You may be thinking to yourself, "Who needs it?" Anybody with a penchant for the different. The exciting. The original.

Why did we do it? To make this the year we win you over to Plymouth.

We've been designing cars with gals in mind for years. Maybe that's why we have the biggest selection of interiors we've ever had.

More colors. More fabrics and vinyls. More choices in seat designs. Maybe that's why we have self-adjusting brakes and optional puncture-resistant tires.

If the print pictured on our Barracuda Sports Coupe doesn't win you over, there is an aqua and blue floral pattern available on Satellite. And there are a number of other features available with women-winning ways.

See your nearby Plymouth dealer. He has a whole mad, mod story to tell this year. And he's out to win you over, too.

Look what Plymouth's up to now.

▲ *It's estimated that just 937 Barracudas were wearing a mod top when they left the factory in 1969.*

Bought originally in ▼ *Des Moines, Iowa, this Barracuda has accumulated just 20,000 miles and two owners in 37-plus years.*

that Plymouth has "been designing cars with gals in mind for years."

By today's standards, the marketing approach seems farfetched, but the Mod Top? That's just "far out!"